HOT & SPICY

HOT & SPICY

A sizzling selection of more than 200 tastebud-tingling recipes from around the world, from hot and fiery to deliciously aromatic, shown step by step in 780 red-hot photographs

Linda Fraser

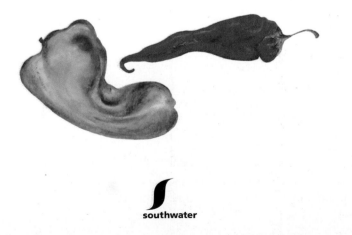

ʃ
southwater

This edition is published by Southwater,
an imprint of Anness Publishing Ltd,
108 Great Russell Street, London WC1B 3NA;
info@anness.com

www.southwaterbooks.com; www.annesspublishing.com

If you like the images in this book and would like to investigate using them for publishing,
promotions or advertising, please visit our website www.practicalpictures.com
for more information

A CIP catalogue record for this book is available from the British Library.

Publisher: Joanna Lorenz
Senior Cookery Editor: Linda Fraser
Project Editor: Anne Hildyard
Designer: Siân Keogh
Book Illustrations: Madeleine David
Photography: William Adams-Lingwood, Karl Adamson, Edward Allwright,
David Armstrong, Steve Baxter, James Duncan, Nelson Hargreaves,
Amanda Heywood, Janine Hosegood, David Jordan, Patrick McLeavey,
Michael Michaels and Thomas Odulate
Recipes: Kit Chan, Jacqueline Clark, Roz Denny, Joanna Farrow, Rafi Fernandez, Christine France, Silvana Franco,
Sarah Gates, Deh-Ta Hsiung, Shehzad Husain, Elizabeth Ortiz Lambert, Sallie Morris, Hilaire Walden, Laura Washburn,
Pamela Westland, Steven Wheeler and Judy Williams
Food for Photography: Carla Capalbo, Kit Chan, Jacqueline Clark, Joanne Craig, Rosamund Grant, Carole Handslip,
Jane Hartshorn, Wendy Lee, Lucy McKelvie, Annie Nichols, Jane Stevenson, Steven Wheeler and Elizabeth Wolf-Cohen
Stylists: Hilary Guy, Clare Hunt, Maria Kelly, Patrick McLeavey, Blake Minton, Thomas Odulate and Kirsty Rawlings

NOTES
Bracketed terms are intended for American readers.
For all recipes, quantities are given in both metric and imperial measures and, where appropriate, in standard cups and
spoons. Follow one set of measures, but not a mixture, because they are not interchangeable.
Standard spoon and cup measures are level. 1 tsp = 5ml, 1 tbsp = 15ml, 1 cup = 250ml/8fl oz.
Australian standard tablespoons are 20ml. Australian readers should use 3 tsp in place of
1 tbsp for measuring small quantities.
American pints are 16fl oz/2 cups. American readers should use 20fl oz/2.5 cups in place of
1 pint when measuring liquids.
Electric oven temperatures in this book are for conventional ovens. When using a fan oven,
the temperature will probably need to be reduced by about 10–20°C/20–40°F.
Since ovens vary, you should check with your manufacturer's instruction book for guidance.
Medium (US large) eggs are used unless otherwise stated.

The consultant editor would like to thank chilli grower Michael Michaud and Christine McFadden, fellow members of the
Guild of Food Writers, for sharing their knowledge and enthusiasm for chillies. Michael and Joy Michaud are market
gardeners, and from July to December each year they can supply fresh chillies by mail order.
Contact them at Peppers by Post, Sea Spring Farm, West Bexington, Dorchester, Dorset DT2 9DD, UK.
Telephone 01308 897898.

CONTENTS

INTRODUCTION

IF VARIETY is the spice of life, it certainly must be said that spices give life – or at least food – its variety.

In all their idiosyncratic guises, spices lend richness, heat and complexity to literally every food imaginable, and it is impossible to conceive of a cuisine that does not benefit from unique and distinctive spicing. In fact, from the sun-drenched Caribbean to the deserts of the Middle East, the dense jungles of Vietnam and Indonesia, the bustling sidewalk stalls of Thailand, the great plains of Africa, the crowded streets of Mexico, and the spirited southwestern United States, "hot and spicy" defines good eating for millions of people who would not dream of consuming bland, unseasoned food when piquant delights are available at

every turn. Attention-grabbing spices are nothing if not highly particular, well-defined and capable of transforming dishes with a single pinch. For example, what would a searing Indian vindaloo taste like without its delicately balanced curry? Or a Thai Beef Salad without the powerful punch of chillies? Blackened Chicken Breasts without Cajun seasonings? Jerk Chicken without Habanero chilli peppers? Probably like King Lear's meat without salt – in other words: not much. Indeed, for thousands of years, the right spice, or combination of spices, has actually helped define individual cultures by lending a nation's or a people's cuisine a flavour and a style that is unmistakably its own. Within these pages you will find an exhilarating, mind-expanding, and palate-tingling

collection of recipes from every corner of the world.

Archaeological evidence shows that the cultivation of chilli peppers thrived among the Aztecs of South America over 2000 years ago. Among Asian cultures, subtle and varied spicing has been prevalent for years. Some gastronomes hold that spicing first became popular in medieval Europe to enhance the keeping qualities and mask the taste and smell of food that had gone rancid in the days before refrigeration. Whatever their original use, spices became one of the most precious and desired commodities on the market – spices such as pepper and cinnamon from lands as far off as Sumatra and Ceylon were traded for land and even used to pay taxes. What is certain is that whatever the origins of spices, we would live – and eat – in a dull world without them. Surely the sensual pleasure of a well-seasoned meal is reason enough to value the spices that make modern dining such an adventure.

With this exciting, exhilarating cookbook in hand, mouth-searing, tongue-teasing meals will explode from your kitchen, energizing and inspiring all those who share with you the most exciting dishes around.

HOT AND SPICY INGREDIENTS

ALLSPICE

Available whole or ground, allspice are small, dark brown berries similar in size to large peppercorns. They can be used in sweet or savoury dishes and have a flavour of nutmeg, cinnamon and clove, hence the name.

CARDAMOM

These pods are green, black and creamy beige, green being the most common. Whole pods are used in rice and meat dishes to add flavour and should not be eaten. Black seeds are used in desserts.

CHILLIES

Chillies are available from greengrocers and supermarkets. They are grown on a dwarf bush with small dense green leaves, white flowers and red or green finger-shaped fruit. In general, the green chilli is less hot and possesses a rather earthy heat. The red chilli is usually hotter and is often very fiery.

To prepare chillies, remove the cap from the stalk end and slit it from top to bottom with a small knife. Under running water, scoop out the seeds with the knife point. The fire comes from the seeds so leave them if you like food to be fiercely hot. Chillies contain volatile oil that can irritate the skin and sting the eyes, so it is best to use rubber gloves when preparing chillies, or wash hands afterwards with soap and water.

There are many different varieties of chillies. The small red and green fresh chillies are known as Thai or bird's eye chillies and are extremely hot. One of the hottest varieties is the fat and fiery Scotch Bonnet or habanero. It has a spicy smell and flavour and can be red, green, yellow or brown. There are innumerable types of chillies that are indigenous to Mexico. The most commonly used fresh green chillies are serrano, jalapeño and poblano. These varieties are all very hot. Anaheim, popular in the US, is milder.

Opposite page: In the spice chest (top right), from the left: cayenne pepper, fennel seeds and ground turmeric. On the table: fresh red and green chillies. In the large bowl: a selection of ingredients for an Indian vegetarian curry: red chillies, aubergines (eggplant), okra, bitter gourds, bay leaves, red (bell) peppers; and in the small bowl: coriander seeds.

Dried chillies are very popular and there are numerous varieties available. The most commonly used dried chillies are ancho, which is full-flavoured and mild; chipotle, a very hot variety; mulato, which is pungent, and the hot pasilla.

CHILLI PRODUCTS

Cayenne pepper is a pungent spicy powder made from a blend of small ripe red chillies.

Chilli powder is made from dried, ground chillies and is often mixed with other spices and herbs.

Chilli flakes are made from dried, crushed chillies and are used in pickles.

Chilli oil is widely used in Chinese cooking. Dried red chillies are heated with vegetable oil to make this hot, pungent condiment.

Chilli paste is a convenient way of adding fiery heat to sauces.

Hot pepper sauce is made from red chillies and vinegar and is used to sprinkle over many dishes.

CINNAMON

Available as bark or in the ground form, cinnamon has a woody aroma with a fragrant and warm flavour. The powdered form is widely used in the Middle East, especially in Khoresh. It is a versatile

From left: fresh, glossy lime leaves, lemon grass and fresh coriander (cilantro) leaves and root.

spice, is good in lamb dishes as well as in spiced drinks, fruit compotes, chocolate cakes and desserts.

CLOVES

Cloves are used in spice mixtures such as garam masala and in many meat and rice dishes. They can also be used to add spicy flavour to fruit and desserts.

CORIANDER

This spice is used throughout the world. It is available as either whole seeds or ground powder. The ripe seeds have a sweet, spicy aroma with a hint of orange flavour. Coriander can be used in both sweet and savoury dishes and is one of the essential ingredients in curry powder. The flavour of coriander can be accentuated by dry-frying.

Coriander (cilantro) leaves are essential in the cooking of South-East Asia and India and the root of the plant is often used in Thai cooking.

CUMIN

Cumin is available as small brown ridged seeds or in the ground form. Both types have a characteristic pungent, warm flavour. Cumin is also often dry-roasted to bring out the flavour. This spice is very popular in the Middle East, where it is used in spice mixtures such as garam masala and is added to pickles and salads. Cumin is one of the main ingredients of curry powder.

CURRY PASTE

Curry pastes are made by pounding spices with red or green chillies. They are ferociously hot and will keep for about 1 month in the refrigerator.

FISH SAUCE

Known as nam pla, this is a commonly used flavouring in Thai dishes in the same way that soy sauce is used in Chinese cooking. Fish sauce is made from salted anchovies and although not a spice, it contributes a depth of pungent salty flavour to any dish.

FIVE-SPICE POWDER

This reddish brown powder is a combination of five ground spices – star anise, fennel, clove, cinnamon and Sichuan pepper. Used sparingly, it has a wonderful flavour, but it can be dominant if too much is added. The spices can also be bought whole in a mixed packet for grinding as needed.

GALANGAL

This is a member of the ginger family and looks rather similar to fresh root ginger. The root is creamy coloured, with a translucent skin that has rings, and may have pink nodules rather like young ginger. It has a refreshing sharp, lemony taste and is best used fresh, although it is available in dried or powder form. If you cannot find fresh galangal, use about 5ml/1tsp of the dried powder to replace each 2.5cm/1in fresh galangal.

To prepare fresh galagal, cut a piece of the required size. Trim off any knobbly bits, then peel carefully, because the tough skin has an unpleasant taste. Slice to use in a paste and use up as soon as possible after peeling, to prevent loss of flavour. The flesh is much more woody and fibrous than ginger and has a distinctive, pine-like smell. Store galangal wrapped, in the salad drawer of the refrigerator.

GARAM MASALA

This spice mixture is made from a variety of spices and can be a simple blend, consisting of two or three spices and herbs, or a more complex masala, made from twelve or more different spices. The dry spices and seeds are often dry-roasted first and sometimes whole spices are used. Garam masala may be added to the dish at different cooking stages.

Clockwise from top left: red chillies, mild, glossy green Kenyan chillies, hot green chillies, green chillies, orange Thai chillies, red bird's eye chillies and green bird's eye chillies.

Clockwise from top left: green jalapeño chillies, large green anaheim chillies, small green chillies, chipotle (smoked dried jalapeño chillies), dried mulato chillies, dried habanero chillies, dried pasilla chillies, green (bell) peppers, and (centre top left) yellow and red Scotch Bonnet chillies, (centre right) fresh red chillies.

GINGER

A root of Chinese and Indian origin with a silvery brown skin, ginger is best used fresh, and should be peeled and chopped or crushed before cooking. It is available in supermarkets – look for shiny smooth fat roots. Store in the salad drawer of the refrigerator, wrapped in kitchen paper. Ginger is a good alternative to galangal in Thai cooking.

LEMON GRASS

This tropical grass has a fresh, highly aromatic lemony taste and is a vital ingredient in South-East Asian cooking. It combines well with garlic and chillies and is pounded to a paste, then added to curries. Unless it is finely chopped, lemon grass is usually removed before serving as it has a very fibrous texture.

LIME LEAVES

These glossy, dark green leaves come from the kaffir lime tree. They have a pleasing, distinctive smell and can be torn or left whole. They can be frozen and used straight from the freezer in curries and sauces.

NUTMEG

Whole nutmegs are the hard aromatic seeds of an evergreen tree. The spice,

Overleaf: hot and spicy ingredients from left to right, from top row:

Whole cloves, dried ground ginger, fresh root ginger and green cardamoms.

Tamarind pulp, whole cumin seeds, garam masala, saffron, garlic, bay leaves and fresh coriander (cilantro).

Whole black mustard seeds, ground cumin, whole nutmeg, black peppercorns, fennel seeds, whole cinnamon sticks and paprika.

Curry leaves, ground turmeric, fresh mint leaves, fenugreek seeds and ground coriander.

Curry powder, sesame seeds, chilli powder, dried red chillies and coriander seeds.

Opposite page: a selection of spices, left to right from top row: paprika, whole green cardamoms, cumin seeds, saffron threads, ground turmeric, whole nutmeg and mace, ground sumac, cinnamon sticks and ground nutmeg.

which has a sweet, nutty flavour, is widely used all over the world. Whole nutmegs can be grated for cooking, but the ground spice is often used, particularly in the Middle East. Nutmeg can be used in both savoury and sweet dishes.

PAPRIKA

This spice is made from a mixture of ground dried red peppers. Both mild and hot peppers are used, but paprika is always milder than cayenne pepper. It is widely used in the Middle East in soups, meat dishes, salad dressings and as a garnish.

PEPPERCORNS

White, green and black peppercorns are berries from the same plant, picked at different stages of maturity, and are used whole and ground. Pepper has a pungent flavour and can be used in either savoury or sweet dishes. Peppercorns can be used whole crushed or ground.

Sichuan pepper is also known as anise pepper. The berries are red-brown in colour and are prickly. They are spicy with a rather numbing taste.

SAFFRON

Made from the dried stamens of a type of crocus, saffron has a superb aroma and flavour. It also adds a delicate yellow colour to food. For the best results it should be ground to a powder and diluted in a small amount of boiling water.

TAMARIND

An acidic-tasting tropical fruit that resembles a bean pod. It is added to curries to give a sharp flavour. Tamarind is usually sold dried or pulped. To make tamarind juice, soak a piece of tamarind pulp in warm water for about 10 minutes. Squeeze out as much tamarind juice as possible by pressing all the liquid through a sieve.

TURMERIC

Turmeric is another member of the ginger family. When the whole spice is peeled or scraped, a rich golden root is revealed. Turmeric adds a distinctive flavour and rich yellow colour to meat and rice dishes. It is widely used throughout the Middle East and India. Because of its strong, bitter flavour, it should be used sparingly.

ZERESHK

This is a small sour berry that comes from Iran. It is traditionally served with Persian rice dishes.

Left: clockwise from left: fresh turmeric roots before being ground to a fine powder, cut to show their vivid golden colour, creamy coloured fresh galangal roots, showing typical rings on the skin and pink nodules, and a large piece of unpeeled fresh ginger root showing the characteristic silvery brown skin.

Soups are always satisfying and warming, and these soups certainly fill the bill. Drawn from Thailand, Africa, India and the Middle East, where chillies and spices are everyday foods, the recipes are a rich mixture of flavourful ingredients, enlivened by the addition of hot pickles, peppers and chillies, as well as aromatic spices. Hot and Spicy Seafood Soup and Mulligatawny Soup are sure to stimulate the appetite.

Spicy Soups

TORTILLA SOUP

INGREDIENTS
15ml/1 tbsp vegetable oil
1 onion, chopped
1 large garlic clove, minced
2 tomatoes, peeled, seeded
  and chopped
2.5ml/$\frac{1}{2}$ tsp salt
2.4 litres/4 pints/10 cups chicken stock
1 carrot, diced
1 small courgette (zucchini), diced
1 skinless boneless chicken breast
  portion, cooked and shredded
6 canned green chillies, chopped

To garnish
4 corn tortillas
oil, for frying
1 small ripe avocado
2 spring onions (scallions), chopped
chopped fresh coriander (cilantro)

1 Heat the oil in a pan. Add the onion and garlic and cook over a medium heat for 5–8 minutes, until just softened. Add the tomatoes and salt and cook for another 5 minutes.

2 Stir in the chicken stock. Bring the liquid to the boil, covered, then lower the heat and simmer for about 15 minutes.

3 Meanwhile, for the garnish, trim the tortillas into squares, then cut into strips.

4 Put a 1cm/$\frac{1}{2}$ in layer of oil in a frying pan and heat until hot but not smoking. Add the tortilla strips, in batches, and fry until just beginning to brown, turning occasionally. Remove with a slotted spoon and drain on kitchen paper.

5 Add the carrot to the soup. Cook, covered, for 10 minutes. Add the courgette, chicken and chillies and continue cooking, uncovered, for about 5 minutes, until the vegetables are just tender.

6 Meanwhile, peel and stone (pit) the avocado. Chop into fine dice.

7 Divide the tortilla strips among four soup bowls and sprinkle each one with the avocado. Ladle in the soup, then sprinkle the onions and coriander on top. Serve immediately.

TAMARIND SOUP WITH PEANUTS AND VEGETABLES

SAYUR ASAM, AS THIS DISH IS ALSO KNOWN, IS A COLOURFUL AND REFRESHING SOUP FROM JAKARTA WITH MORE THAN A HINT OF SHARPNESS.

SERVES 4 OR 8 AS PART OF A BUFFET

INGREDIENTS
For the spice paste
   5 shallots or 1 medium red
      onion, sliced
   3 garlic cloves, crushed
   2.5cm/1in galangal, peeled and sliced
   1–2 fresh red chillies, seeded and sliced
   25g/1oz/$\frac{1}{4}$ cup raw peanuts
   1cm/$\frac{1}{2}$in cube shrimp paste, prepared
   1.2 litres/2 pints/5 cups well-
      flavoured stock
   50–75g/2–3oz/$\frac{1}{2}$–$\frac{3}{4}$ cup salted
      peanuts, lightly crushed
   15–30ml/1–2 tbsp dark brown sugar
   5ml/1 tsp tamarind pulp, soaked in
      75ml/5 tbsp warm water for
      15 minutes
salt

For the vegetables
   1 chayote, thinly peeled, seeds
      removed, flesh finely sliced
   115g/4oz/$\frac{3}{4}$ cup green beans, trimmed
      and finely sliced
   50g/2oz/$\frac{1}{3}$ cup corn kernels (optional)
   handful green leaves, such as
      watercress, rocket (arugula) or
      Chinese leaves (Chinese cabbage),
      finely shredded
   1 fresh green chilli, sliced, to garnish

2 Pour in some of the stock to moisten and then pour this mixture into a pan or wok, adding the rest of the stock. Cook for 15 minutes with the lightly crushed peanuts and sugar.

5 Add the tamarind juice and taste for seasoning. Serve, garnished with slices of green chilli.

1 Prepare the spice paste by grinding the shallots or onion, garlic, galangal, chillies, raw peanuts and shrimp paste to a paste in a food processor or using a mortar and pestle.

3 Strain the tamarind, discarding the seeds, and reserve the juice.

4 About 5 minutes before serving, add the chayote slices, beans and corn, if using, to the soup and cook fairly rapidly. At the last minute, add the green leaves and salt to taste.

PUMPKIN AND CHILLI SOUP

SERVES 4–6

INGREDIENTS

2 garlic cloves, crushed
4 shallots, finely chopped
2.5ml/^{1}/$_2$ tsp shrimp paste
15ml/1 tbsp dried shrimp soaked for
  10 minutes and drained
1 lemon grass stalk, chopped
2 green chillies, seeded
600ml/1 pint/2^1/$_2$ cups chicken stock
450g/1lb pumpkin, cut into 2cm/^{3}/$_4$ in
  thick chunks
600ml/1 pint/2^1/$_2$ cups coconut cream
30ml/2 tbsp fish sauce
5ml/1 tsp granulated sugar
115g/4oz/1 cup small cooked peeled
  prawns (shrimp)
salt and ground black pepper
2 red chillies, seeded and finely
  sliced, and 10–12 basil leaves,
  to garnish

1 Grind the garlic, shallots, shrimp paste, dried shrimp, lemon grass, green chillies and salt into a paste.

2 In a large pan, bring the chicken stock to the boil, add the ground paste and stir to dissolve.

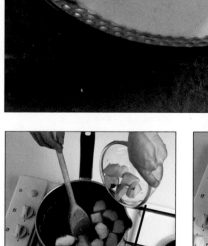

3 Add the pumpkin and simmer for about 10–15 minutes or until the pumpkin is tender.

4 Stir in the coconut cream, then bring back to a simmer. Add the fish sauce, sugar and ground black pepper to taste.

5 Add the prawns and cook until they are heated through. Serve garnished with the sliced red chillies and basil leaves.

COOK'S TIP
Shrimp paste, which is made from ground shrimp fermented in brine, is used to give food a savoury flavour.

SPICY VEGETABLE SOUP

<u>SERVES 4</u>

INGREDIENTS
$^1/_2$ red onion
175g/6oz each, turnip, sweet potato
  and pumpkin
30ml/2 tbsp butter or margarine
5ml/1 tsp dried marjoram
2.5ml/$^1/_2$ tsp ground ginger
1.5ml/$^1/_4$ tsp ground cinnamon
15ml/1 tbsp chopped spring onion (scallion)
1 litre/1$^3/_4$ pint/4 cups well-flavoured
  vegetable stock
30ml/2 tbsp flaked (sliced) almonds
1 fresh chilli, seeded and chopped
5ml/1 tsp sugar
25g/1oz creamed coconut
salt and ground black pepper
chopped coriander (cilantro), to garnish

1 Finely chop the onion, then peel the turnip, sweet potato and pumpkin and chop into medium dice.

2 Melt the butter or margarine in a large non-stick pan. Cook the onion for about 4–5 minutes. Add the diced vegetables and cook for 3–4 minutes.

3 Add the marjoram, ginger, cinnamon, spring onion, salt and pepper. Cook over a low heat for about 10 minutes, stirring frequently.

4 Add the vegetable stock, flaked almonds, chopped chilli and sugar and stir well to mix, then cover and simmer gently for 10–15 minutes until the vegetables are just tender.

5 Grate the creamed coconut into the soup and stir to mix. Sprinkle with chopped coriander, if you like, spoon into warmed bowls and serve.

PLANTAIN SOUP WITH CORN AND CHILLI

SERVES 4

INGREDIENTS

25g/1oz/2 tbsp butter or margarine
1 onion, finely chopped
1 garlic clove, crushed
275g/10oz yellow plantains, peeled
  and sliced
1 large tomato, peeled and chopped
175g/6oz/1 cup corn kernels
5ml/1 tsp dried tarragon, crushed
900ml/1^{1}/2pints/3^{3}/4 cups vegetable or
  chicken stock
1 green chilli, seeded and chopped
pinch of grated nutmeg
salt and ground black pepper

1 Melt the butter or margarine in a pan over a medium heat, add the onion and garlic and cook for a few minutes until the onion is soft.

2 Add the plantain, tomato and corn and cook for 5 minutes.

3 Add the tarragon, vegetable stock, chilli and salt and pepper and simmer for 10 minutes, or until the plantain is tender. Stir in the nutmeg and serve immediately.

SPICY GROUNDNUT SOUP

THIS SOUP IS WIDELY EATEN IN AFRICA. GROUNDNUTS (OR PEANUTS) ARE SPICED WITH A MIXTURE OF FRESH GINGER AND CHILLI POWDER WITH HERBS ADDED FOR EXTRA FLAVOUR. THE AMOUNT OF CHILLI POWDER CAN BE VARIED ACCORDING TO TASTE, ADD MORE FOR A FIERY HOT SOUP.

SERVES 4

INGREDIENTS

45ml/3 tbsp pure groundnut (peanut)
  paste or peanut butter
1.5 litres/2^{1}/2 pints/6^{1}/4 cups stock
  or water
30ml/2 tbsp tomato purée (paste)
1 onion, chopped
2 slices fresh root ginger
1.5ml/^{1}/4 tsp dried thyme
1 bay leaf
salt and chilli powder
225g/8oz white yam, diced
10 small okra, trimmed (optional)

1 Place the groundnut paste or peanut butter in a bowl, add 300ml/^{1}/2 pint/1^{1}/4 cups of the stock or water and the tomato purée and blend together to make a smooth paste.

2 Spoon the nut mixture into a pan and add the onion, ginger, thyme, bay leaf, salt, chilli and the remaining stock.

3 Heat gently until simmering, then cook for 1 hour, stirring occasionally to prevent the nut mixture from sticking.

4 Add the white yam, cook for a further 10 minutes, and then add the okra, if using, and simmer until both are tender. Serve immediately.

BEEF AND TURMERIC SOUP

THE ADDITION OF TURMERIC AND SAFFRON COLOURS THIS SATISFYING SOUP A DEEP, VIBRANT YELLOW. IT IS A POPULAR DISH IN IRAN.

SERVES 6

INGREDIENTS

2 large onions
30ml/2 tbsp oil
15ml/1 tbsp ground turmeric
100g/3^1/2oz/^{1}/2 cup yellow split peas
1.2 litres/2 pints/5 cups water
225g/8oz/2 cups minced (ground) beef
200g/7oz/1 cup rice
45ml/3 tbsp each fresh chopped
   parsley, coriander (cilantro) and
   chives
15g/^{1}/2 oz/1 tbsp butter
1 large garlic clove, finely chopped
60ml/4 tbsp chopped fresh mint
2–3 saffron threads dissolved in
   15ml/1 tbsp boiling water (optional)
salt and ground black pepper
yogurt and naan bread, to serve

1 Chop one of the onions, then heat the oil in a large pan and cook the onion until golden brown. Add the turmeric, split peas and water, bring to the boil, then reduce the heat and simmer for 20 minutes.

COOK'S TIP
Fresh spinach is also delicious in this soup. Add 50g/2oz/^{2}/3 cup finely chopped spinach leaves to the soup with the parsley, coriander (cilantro) and chives.

2 Grate the other onion into a bowl, add the minced beef and seasoning and mix well. Using your hands, form the mixture into small balls, about the size of walnuts. Carefully add to the pan and simmer for 10 minutes.

3 Add the rice, then stir in the parsley, coriander, and chives and simmer for about 30 minutes, until the rice is tender, stirring frequently.

4 Melt the butter in a small pan and gently cook the garlic for 2–3 minutes, ensuring that it does not burn. Add the mint, stir briefly and sprinkle over the soup with the saffron, if using.

5 Spoon the soup into warmed serving dishes and serve, accompanied by yogurt and naan bread.

MULLIGATAWNY SOUP

MULLIGATAWNY (WHICH MEANS "PEPPER WATER") WAS INTRODUCED INTO ENGLAND IN THE LATE EIGHTEENTH CENTURY BY MEMBERS OF THE ARMY AND COLONIAL SERVICE RETURNING HOME FROM INDIA.

SERVES 4

INGREDIENTS

50g/2oz/4 tbsp butter or
  60ml/4 tbsp oil
2 large chicken portions, about
  350g/12oz each
1 onion, chopped
1 carrot, chopped
1 small turnip, chopped
about 15ml/1 tbsp curry powder,
  to taste
4 cloves
6 black peppercorns, lightly crushed
50g/2oz/$^{1}/_{4}$ cup lentils
900ml/1$^{1}/_{2}$ pints/3$^{3}/_{4}$ cups chicken
  stock
40g/1$^{1}/_{2}$ oz/$^{1}/_{4}$ cup sultanas
  (golden raisins)
salt and ground black pepper

1 Melt the butter or heat the oil in a large pan, then brown the chicken over a brisk heat. Transfer the chicken to a plate.

2 Add the chopped onion, carrot and turnip to the pan and cook, stirring occasionally, until they are lightly coloured. Stir in the curry powder, cloves and black peppercorns and cook for 1–2 minutes more before adding the lentils.

3 Pour the stock into the pan, bring to the boil, then add the sultanas and chicken and any juices from the plate. Cover and simmer gently for about 1$^{1}/_{4}$ hours.

4 Remove the chicken from the pan and discard the skin and bones. Chop the flesh, return to the soup and reheat. Check the seasoning before serving the soup piping hot.

COOK'S TIP
Choose red split lentils for the best colour, although either green or brown lentils could also be used.

SPICY YOGURT SOUP

<u>SERVES 4–6</u>

INGREDIENTS

450ml/³/4 pint/scant 2 cups natural
  (plain) yogurt, beaten
60ml/4 tbsp gram flour
2.5ml/¹/2 tsp chilli powder
2.5ml/¹/2 tsp ground turmeric
2–3 green chillies, finely chopped
60ml/4 tbsp vegetable oil
4 whole dried red chillies
5ml/1 tsp cumin seeds
3–4 curry leaves
3 garlic cloves, crushed
5cm/2in piece of fresh root
  ginger, crushed
salt
fresh coriander (cilantro) leaves,
  chopped, to garnish

1 Mix together the yogurt, gram flour, chilli powder, turmeric and salt and strain them into a pan. Add the green chillies and cook gently for about 10 minutes, stirring occasionally. Be careful not to let the soup boil over.

2 Heat the oil in a frying pan and fry the remaining spices, crushed garlic and fresh ginger until the dried chillies turn black.

3 Pour the oil and the spices over the yogurt soup, remove the pan from the heat, cover and leave to rest for 5 minutes. Mix well and gently reheat for a further 5 minutes. Serve hot, garnished with the coriander leaves.

VARIATION
Sugar can be added to this soup to bring out the full flavour. For an extra creamy soup, use Greek (US strained plain) yogurt instead of natural (plain) yogurt. Adjust the amount of chillies according to how hot you want the soup to be.

HOT AND SPICY SEAFOOD SOUP

FOR A SPECIAL OCCASION SERVE CREAMY RICE NOODLES IN A SPICY COCONUT-FLAVOURED SOUP, TOPPED WITH SEAFOOD. THERE IS A FAIR AMOUNT OF WORK INVOLVED IN THE PREPARATION BUT YOU CAN MAKE THE SOUP BASE AHEAD.

SERVES 4

INGREDIENTS

4 red chillies, seeded and
  roughly chopped
1 onion, coarsely chopped
1 small piece shrimp paste
1 lemon grass stalk, chopped
1 small piece fresh root ginger,
  coarsely chopped
6 macadamia nuts or almonds
60ml/4 tbsp vegetable oil
5ml/1 tsp paprika
5ml/1 tsp ground turmeric
475ml/16fl oz/2 cups stock or water
600ml/1 pint/2^1/$_2$ cups coconut milk
fish sauce (see method)
12 king prawns (jumbo shrimp), peeled
  and deveined
8 scallops
225g/8oz prepared squid, cut into rings
350g/12oz rice vermicelli or rice
  noodles, soaked in warm water
  until soft
salt and ground black pepper
lime halves, to serve

For the garnish
  ^{1}/$_4$ cucumber, cut into sticks
  2 red chillies, seeded and finely sliced
  30ml/2 tbsp fresh mint leaves
  30ml/2 tbsp fried shallots or onions

1 In a blender or food processor, process the chillies, onion, shrimp paste, lemon grass, ginger and nuts until smooth in texture.

2 Heat 45ml/3 tbsp of the oil in a large pan. Add the chilli paste and cook for 6 minutes. Stir in the paprika and turmeric and cook for about 2 minutes more.

3 Add the stock or water and the coconut milk to the pan. Bring to the boil, reduce the heat and simmer gently for 15–20 minutes. Season to taste with fish sauce.

4 Season the seafood with salt and pepper. Heat the remaining oil in a frying pan, add the seafood and cook quickly for 2–3 minutes until tender.

5 Add the noodles to the soup and heat through. Divide among individual serving bowls. Place the seafood on top, then garnish with the cucumber, chillies, mint and fried shallots or onions. Serve with the limes.

COOK'S TIP
Dried shrimp is sold in small blocks and you will find it in Asian stores and supermarkets.

GINGER, CHICKEN AND COCONUT SOUP

THIS AROMATIC SOUP IS RICH WITH COCONUT MILK AND INTENSELY FLAVOURED WITH GALANGAL, LEMON GRASS AND KAFFIR LIME LEAVES.

SERVES 4–6

INGREDIENTS

750ml/1¼ pints/3 cups coconut milk
475ml/16fl oz/2 cups chicken stock
4 lemon grass stalks, bruised and chopped
2.5cm/1in piece galangal, thinly sliced
10 black peppercorns, crushed
10 kaffir lime leaves, torn
300g/11oz boneless chicken, cut
    into thin strips
115g/4oz/1²/₃ cups button
    (white) mushrooms
50g/2oz baby corn
60ml/4 tbsp lime juice
45ml/3 tbsp fish sauce
2 red chillies, chopped, chopped spring
    onions (scallions) and coriander
    (cilantro) leaves, to garnish

1 Bring the coconut milk and chicken stock to the boil. Add the lemon grass, galangal, peppercorns and half the kaffir lime leaves, reduce the heat and simmer gently for 10 minutes.

3 Stir in the lime juice, fish sauce to taste and the rest of the lime leaves. Serve hot, garnished with red chillies, spring onions and coriander.

2 Strain the stock into a clean pan. Return to the heat, then add the chicken, button mushrooms and baby corn. Cook for about 5–7 minutes, or until the chicken is cooked.

HOT AND SOUR PRAWN SOUP WITH LEMON GRASS

THIS IS A CLASSIC THAI SEAFOOD SOUP – TOM YAM GOONG – AND IS PROBABLY THE MOST POPULAR AND BEST KNOWN SOUP FROM THAILAND.

SERVES 4–6

INGREDIENTS

450g/1lb king prawns (jumbo shrimp)
1 litre/1³/₄ pints/4 cups chicken stock
    or water
3 lemon grass stalks
10 kaffir lime leaves, torn in half
225g/8oz can straw mushrooms,
    drained
45ml/3 tbsp fish sauce
50ml/2fl oz/¼ cup lime juice
30ml/2 tbsp chopped spring
    onion (scallion)
15ml/1 tbsp coriander (cilantro)
    leaves
4 red chillies, seeded and chopped
2 spring onions, finely chopped

1 Peel and devein the prawns and set aside. Rinse the prawn shells and place in a large pan with the stock or water and bring to the boil.

2 Bruise the lemon grass stalks with the blunt edge of a chopping knife and add them to the stock together with half of the lime leaves. Simmer gently for 5–6 minutes, until the stalks change colour and the stock is fragrant.

3 Strain the stock, return to the pan and reheat. Add the mushrooms and prawns, then cook until the prawns turn pink.

4 Stir in the fish sauce, lime juice, spring onions, coriander, red chillies and the rest of the lime leaves. Taste and adjust the seasoning. It should be sour, salty, spicy and hot.

SPICED LAMB SOUP

SERVES 4

INGREDIENTS

115g/4oz/²/₃ cup split black-eyed
   beans (peas), soaked for 1–2 hours,
   or overnight
675g/1¹/₂ lb neck (US shoulder) of
   lamb, cut into medium chunks
5ml/1 tsp chopped fresh thyme, or
   2.5ml/¹/₂ tsp dried
2 bay leaves
1.2 litres/2 pints/5 cups stock or water
1 onion, sliced
225g/8oz pumpkin, diced
2 black cardamom pods
7.5ml/1¹/₂ tsp ground turmeric
15ml/1 tbsp chopped coriander
   (cilantro)
2.5ml/¹/₂ tsp caraway seeds
1 fresh green chilli, seeded and chopped
 2 green bananas
1 carrot
salt and ground black pepper

1 Drain the black-eyed beans, place them
in a pan and cover with fresh cold water.

2 Bring the beans to the boil, boil rapidly
for 10 minutes and then reduce the heat
and simmer, covered for 40–50 minutes,
until tender, adding more water if
necessary. Remove from the heat and set
aside to cool.

3 Meanwhile, put the lamb in a large pan,
add the thyme, bay leaves and stock or
water and bring to the boil. Cover and
simmer over a medium heat for 1 hour,
until tender.

4 Add the onion, pumpkin, cardamoms,
turmeric, coriander, caraway, chilli and
seasoning and stir. Bring back to a
simmer and then cook, uncovered, for
15 minutes, until the pumpkin is tender,
stirring occasionally.

5 When the beans are cool, spoon into a
blender or food processor with their liquid
and blend to a smooth purée.

6 Cut the bananas into medium slices and
the carrot into thin slices. Stir into the
soup with the beans and cook for 10–12
minutes, until the vegetables are tender.
Adjust the seasoning and serve.

SPICY PEPPER SOUP

THIS IS A HIGHLY SOOTHING BROTH FOR WINTER EVENINGS, ALSO KNOWN AS MULLA-GA-TANI. SERVE WITH THE WHOLE SPICES, OR STRAIN AND REHEAT IF YOU LIKE. THE LEMON JUICE MAY BE ADJUSTED TO TASTE, BUT THIS DISH SHOULD BE DISTINCTLY SOUR.

SERVES 4–6

INGREDIENTS
    30ml/2 tbsp vegetable oil
    2.5ml/$^1/_2$ tsp ground black pepper
    5ml/1 tsp cumin seeds
    2.5ml/$^1/_2$ tsp mustard seeds
    1.5ml/$^1/_4$ tsp asafoetida
    2 whole dried red chillies
    4–6 curry leaves
    2.5ml/$^1/_2$ tsp ground turmeric
    2 garlic cloves, crushed
    300ml/$^1/_2$ pint/1$^1/_4$ cups tomato juice
    juice of 2 lemons
    120ml/4fl oz/$^1/_2$ cup water
    salt, to taste
    coriander (cilantro) leaves, chopped,
      to garnish

VARIATION
If you prefer, use lime juice instead of lemon juice. Add 5ml/1 tsp tamarind paste for extra sourness.

1 In a large pan, heat the oil and fry the ground black pepper, cumin and mustard seeds, asafoetida, red chillies, curry leaves, turmeric and garlic until the chillies are nearly black and the garlic is golden brown.

2 Lower the heat and add the tomato juice, lemon juice, water and salt. Bring the soup to the boil, then simmer gently for about 10 minutes. Pour the soup into bowls, garnish with the chopped coriander and serve.

NOODLE SOUP WITH PORK AND SZECHUAN PICKLE

<u>SERVES 4</u>

INGREDIENTS

1 litre/1³/4 pints/4 cups chicken stock
350g/12oz egg noodles
15ml/1 tbsp dried shrimp, soaked
  in water
30ml/2 tbsp vegetable oil
225g/8oz lean pork,
  finely shredded
15ml/1 tbsp yellow bean paste
15ml/1 tbsp soy sauce
115g/4oz Sichuan hot pickle, rinsed,
  drained and shredded
pinch of sugar
salt and ground black pepper
2 spring onions (scallions), finely
  sliced, to garnish

1 Bring the stock to the boil in a large pan. Add the noodles and cook until almost tender. Drain the dried shrimp, rinse them under cold water, drain again and add to the stock. Lower the heat and simmer for a further 2 minutes. Keep hot. Heat the oil in a frying pan or wok. Add the pork and stir-fry over a high heat for about 3 minutes.

2 Add the bean paste and soy sauce to the pork; stir-fry for 1 minute more. Add the hot pickle with a pinch of sugar. Stir-fry for 1 minute more.

3 Divide the noodles and soup among individual serving bowls. Spoon the pork mixture on top, then sprinkle with the spring onions and serve immediately.

SNAPPER, TOMATO AND TAMARIND NOODLE SOUP

TAMARIND GIVES THIS LIGHT, FRAGRANT NOODLE SOUP A SLIGHTLY SOUR TASTE.

<u>SERVES 4</u>

INGREDIENTS

2 litres/3¹/2 pints/8 cups water
1kg/2¹/4lb red snapper (or other red
  fish such as mullet)
1 onion, sliced
50g/2oz tamarind pods
15ml/1 tbsp fish sauce
15ml/1 tbsp sugar
30ml/2 tbsp vegetable oil
2 garlic cloves, finely chopped
2 lemon grass stalks, very
  finely chopped
4 ripe tomatoes, coarsely chopped
30ml/2 tbsp yellow bean paste
225g/8oz rice vermicelli, soaked in
  warm water until soft
115g/4oz/2 cups beansprouts
8–10 fresh basil or mint sprigs
25g/1oz/¹/4 cup roasted peanuts,
  ground
salt and ground black pepper

1 Bring the water to the boil in a pan. Lower the heat and add the fish and onion, with 2.5ml/¹/2 tsp salt. Simmer gently until the fish is cooked through.

2 Remove the fish from the stock; set aside. Add the tamarind, fish sauce and sugar to the stock. Cook for 5 minutes, then strain the stock into a large jug (pitcher) or bowl. Carefully remove all of the bones from the fish, keeping the flesh in big pieces.

3 Heat the oil in a large frying pan. Add the garlic and lemon grass and cook for a few seconds. Stir in the tomatoes and bean paste. Cook gently for 5–7 minutes, until the tomatoes are soft. Add the stock, bring back to a simmer and adjust the seasoning to taste.

4 Drain the vermicelli. Plunge it into a pan of boiling water for a few minutes, drain and divide among individual serving bowls. Add the beansprouts, fish, basil or mint, and sprinkle the ground peanuts on top. Top up each bowl with the hot soup.

CHICKEN MULLIGATAWNY

SERVES 4–6

INGREDIENTS
    900g/2lb chicken, boned and skinned
    600ml/1 pint/2$^{1}/_{2}$ cups water
    6 green cardamom pods
    5cm/2in piece of cinnamon stick
    4–6 curry leaves
    15ml/1 tbsp ground coriander
    5ml/1 tsp ground cumin
    2.5ml/$^{1}/_{2}$ tsp ground turmeric
    3 garlic cloves, crushed
    12 whole peppercorns
    4 cloves
    1 onion, finely chopped
    115g/4oz coconut cream
    juice of 2 lemons
    salt
    deep-fried onions and coriander
      (cilantro) leaves, chopped, to garnish

1 Cut the chicken into pieces, then place it in a large pan with the water and cook until the chicken is tender. Skim the surface, then strain, reserving the stock and keeping the chicken pieces warm.

2 Return the chicken stock to the pan and reheat. Add the cardamom pods, cinnamon stick, curry leaves, coriander, cumin, turmeric, garlic, peppercorns, cloves, chopped onion, coconut cream, lemon juice and salt to the pan. Simmer for 10–15 minutes, then strain to remove the whole spices and return the chicken to the soup. Reheat the soup, garnish with deep-fried onions and chopped coriander and serve.

COOK'S TIP
For a fast version of this soup, use ready-cooked chicken. Remove any skin and bone and chop into cubes. Add to the soup just before serving, then reheat.

CURRIED NOODLE AND CHICKEN SOUP

HOT RED CURRY PASTE, COCONUT MILK, LIME AND RED CHILLIES ARE USED TO FLAVOUR THIS DELICIOUSLY HOT AND SPICY CHICKEN SOUP, WHICH ORIGINATED IN BURMA.

SERVES 4–6

INGREDIENTS

600ml/1 pint/2¹/₂ cups coconut milk
30ml/2 tbsp red curry paste
5ml/1 tsp ground turmeric
450g/1lb chicken thighs, boned and
  cut into bitesize chunks
600ml/1 pint/2¹/₂ cups chicken stock
60ml/4 tbsp fish sauce
15ml/1 tbsp dark soy sauce
salt and ground black pepper
juice of ¹/₂–1 lime
450g/1lb fresh egg noodles, blanched
  briefly in boiling water

For the garnish

3 spring onions (scallions), chopped
4 red chillies, chopped
4 shallots, chopped
60ml/4 tbsp sliced pickled mustard
  leaves, rinsed
30ml/2 tbsp fried sliced garlic
coriander (cilantro) leaves
4 fried noodle nests (optional)

1 In a large pan, heat about one-third of the coconut milk and bring to the boil, stirring frequently with a wooden spoon until it separates.

2 Add the curry paste and ground turmeric, stir to mix completely and cook until fragrant.

3 Add the chicken and stir-fry for about 2 minutes, checking that all the chunks are coated with the paste.

4 Add the remaining coconut milk, chicken stock, fish sauce and soy sauce. Season with salt and pepper to taste. Simmer gently for 7–10 minutes. Remove from the heat and stir in the lime juice.

5 Reheat the noodles in boiling water, drain and divide among individual bowls. Divide the chicken among the bowls and ladle in the hot soup. Top each serving with a few of each of the garnishes.

Appetizers and snacks offer lots of highly spiced,

mouth-watering morsels and searingly hot bites. Spicy Kebabs set

the taste buds tingling, while Samosas and Seafood Wontons with

Spicy Dressing are perfect to hand around at a drinks party for a

quick spicy appetizer. Start off a meal in lively style with

Chillied Monkfish Parcels.

Sizzling Appetizers
and Snacks

BUTTERFLIED PRAWNS IN CHILLI CHOCOLATE

ALTHOUGH THE COMBINATION OF HOT AND SWEET FLAVOURS MAY SEEM ODD, THIS IS A DELICIOUS APPETIZER. THE USE OF BITTER CHOCOLATE ADDS RICHNESS WITHOUT INCREASING THE SWEETNESS.

SERVES 4

INGREDIENTS

8 large raw prawns (shrimp), in the
   shell
15ml/1 tbsp seasoned flour
15ml/1 tbsp dry sherry
juice of 4 clementines or 1 large
   orange
15g/$\frac{1}{2}$ oz unsweetened dark
   (bittersweet) chocolate, chopped
30ml/2 tbsp olive oil
2 garlic cloves, finely chopped
2.5cm/1in piece fresh root ginger,
   finely chopped
1 small red chilli, seeded and chopped
salt and ground black pepper

1 Peel the prawns, leaving just the tail sections intact. Make a shallow cut down the back of each prawn and carefully pull out and discard the dark intestinal tract. Turn over the prawns so that the undersides are uppermost, then carefully split them open from tail to top, using a small sharp knife, cutting almost, but not quite, through to the back.

2 Press the prawns down firmly to flatten them out. Coat with the seasoned flour and set aside.

3 Gently heat the sherry and clementine or orange juice in a small pan. When warm, remove from the heat and stir in the chopped chocolate until melted.

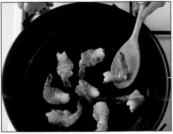

4 Heat the olive oil in a frying pan. Cook the garlic, ginger and chilli over a medium heat for 2 minutes, until golden. Remove with a slotted spoon and reserve. Add the prawns, cut side down, to the pan; cook for 2–3 minutes, until golden brown with pink edges. Turn and cook for a further 2 minutes.

5 Return the garlic mixture to the pan and pour over the chocolate sauce. Cook for 1 minute, turning the prawns to coat them in the glossy sauce. Season to taste and serve hot.

SPICY POTATOES

Spicy potatoes, patatas picantes, are among the most popular tapas dishes in Spain, where they are sometimes described as patatas bravas *(wild potatoes). There are many variations of this classic: boiled new potatoes or large wedges of fried potato may be used, but they are perhaps best simply roasted as in this recipe.*

SERVES 2-4

INGREDIENTS

225g/8oz small new potatoes
15ml/1 tbsp olive oil
5ml/1 tsp paprika
5ml/1 tsp chilli powder
2.5ml/¹/2 tsp ground cumin
2.5ml/¹/2 tsp salt
flat leaf parsley, to garnish

1 Preheat the oven to 200°C/400°F/Gas 6. Prick the skin of each potato in several places with a fork, then place them in a bowl.

2 Add the olive oil, paprika, chilli, cumin and salt and toss well.

COOK'S TIP
This dish is delicious served with tomato sauce or Fiery Salsa – provide small forks for dipping.

3 Transfer the potatoes to a roasting pan and bake for 40 minutes.

4 During cooking, remove the potatoes from the oven and turn them occasionally, until tender. Serve hot, garnished with flat leaf parsley.

FALAFEL

THESE TASTY DEEP FRIED PATTIES ARE ONE OF THE NATIONAL DISHES OF EGYPT. THEY MAKE AN EXCELLENT APPETIZER OR ELSE CAN BE SERVED AS A BUFFET DISH.

SERVES 6

INGREDIENTS

450g/1lb/2^1/$_2$ cups dried white beans
2 red onions, chopped
2 large garlic cloves, crushed
45ml/3 tbsp finely chopped
  fresh parsley
5ml/1 tsp ground coriander
5ml/1 tsp ground cumin
7.5ml/1^1/$_2$ tsp baking powder
oil, for deep-frying
salt and ground black pepper
tomato salad, to serve

1 Soak the white beans overnight in water. Remove the skins and process in a blender or food processor. Add the chopped onions, garlic, parsley, coriander, cumin, baking powder and seasoning and blend again to make a very smooth paste. Leave the mixture to stand at room temperature for at least 30 minutes.

2 Take walnut-size pieces of mixture and flatten into small patties. Set aside again for about 15 minutes.

3 Heat the oil until it's very hot and then fry the patties in batches until golden brown. Drain on kitchen paper and then serve with a tomato salad.

HUMMUS

THIS POPULAR MIDDLE EASTERN DIP IS WIDELY AVAILABLE IN SUPERMARKETS, BUT NOTHING COMPARES WITH THE DELICIOUS HOME-MADE VARIETY.

SERVES 4–6

INGREDIENTS

175g/6oz/1 cup cooked chickpeas
120ml/4fl oz/^{1}/$_2$ cup tahini paste
3 garlic cloves
juice of 2 lemons
45–60ml/3–4 tbsp water
salt and ground black pepper
fresh radishes, to serve

For the garnish
15ml/1 tbsp olive oil
15ml/1 tbsp finely chopped
  fresh parsley
2.5ml/^{1}/$_2$ tsp cayenne pepper
4 black olives

COOK'S TIP
Canned chickpeas can be used for hummus. Drain and rinse under cold water before processing.

1 Place the chickpeas, tahini paste, garlic, lemon juice, seasoning and a little of the water in a blender or food processor. Process until smooth adding a little more water, if necessary.

2 Alternatively, if you don't have a blender or food processor, mix the ingredients together in a small bowl until smooth.

3 Spoon the mixture into a shallow dish. Make a dent in the middle and pour the olive oil into it. Garnish with parsley, cayenne pepper and olives and serve with the radishes.

SAN FRANCISCO CHICKEN WINGS

<u>SERVES 4</u>

INGREDIENTS

75ml/5 tbsp soy sauce
15ml/1 tbsp light brown sugar
15ml/1 tbsp rice vinegar
30ml/2 tbsp dry sherry
juice of 1 orange
5cm/2in strip of orange rind
1 star anise
5ml/1 tsp cornflour (cornstarch)
50ml/2fl oz/¼ cup water
15ml/1 tbsp chopped fresh
  root ginger
5ml/1 tsp chilli-garlic sauce, to taste
1.5kg/3–3½lb chicken wings,
  tips removed

1 Preheat the oven to 200°C/400°F/Gas 6. Mix the soy sauce, sugar, vinegar, sherry, orange juice and rind and anise in a pan. Bring to the boil.

2 Combine the cornflour and water in a small bowl and stir until blended. Add to the boiling soy sauce mixture, stirring well. Boil for another minute, stirring constantly.

3 Remove the soy sauce mixture from the heat and stir in the ginger and chilli-garlic sauce.

4 Arrange the chicken wings, in one layer, in a large ovenproof dish. Pour over the soy sauce mixture and stir to coat the wings evenly.

5 Bake in the centre of the oven for 30–40 minutes, until the chicken wings are tender and browned, basting occasionally. Serve the chicken wings either hot or warm.

CAJUN "POPCORN"

CORNMEAL-COATED SPICY SEAFOOD RESEMBLES POPCORN WHEN MADE, HENCE THE NAME FOR THIS TASTY CAJUN SNACK SERVED WITH A DELICIOUS BASIL MAYONNAISE.

SERVES 8

INGREDIENTS

900g/2lb raw crayfish tails, peeled,
  or small prawns (shrimp),
  peeled and deveined
2 eggs
250ml/8fl oz/1 cup dry white wine
50g/2oz/¹/₂ cup fine cornmeal (or plain
  (all-purpose) flour, if not available)
50g/2oz/¹/₂ cup plain flour
15ml/1 tbsp chopped fresh chives
1 garlic clove, crushed
2.5ml/¹/₂ tsp fresh thyme leaves
1.5ml/¹/₄ tsp salt
1.5ml/¹/₄ tsp cayenne pepper
1.5ml/¹/₄ tsp ground black pepper
oil, for deep-frying

For the mayonnaise
1 egg yolk
10ml/2 tsp Dijon mustard
15ml/1 tbsp white wine vinegar
250ml/8fl oz/1 cup olive or vegetable oil
15g/¹/₂ oz/¹/₂ cup fresh basil
  leaves, chopped
salt and ground black pepper

1 Rinse the crayfish tails or prawns in cold water. Drain well and set aside in a cool place.

2 Mix together the eggs and wine in a small bowl.

3 In a mixing bowl, combine the cornmeal and/or flour, chives, garlic, thyme, salt, cayenne and pepper. Gradually whisk in the egg mixture, blending well. Cover the batter and stand for 1 hour at room temperature.

4 For the mayonnaise, combine the egg yolk, mustard and vinegar in a mixing bowl and add salt and pepper to taste. Add the oil in a thin stream, beating vigorously with a wire whisk. When the mixture is thick and smooth, stir in the basil. Cover and chill until ready to serve.

5 Heat 7.5cm/3in of oil in a large frying pan or deep-fryer to a temperature of 180°C/350°F. Dip the seafood into the batter and fry in small batches for 2–3 minutes, until golden brown. Turn as necessary for even colouring. Remove with a slotted spoon and drain on kitchen paper. Serve hot, with the basil mayonnaise.

MIXED TOSTADAS

LIKE LITTLE EDIBLE PLATES, THESE FRIED TORTILLAS CAN SUPPORT ANYTHING THAT IS NOT TOO JUICY.

MAKES 14

INGREDIENTS
  oil, for shallow frying
  14 freshly prepared unbaked
    corn tortillas
  225g/8oz/1 cup mashed red kidney or
    pinto beans
  1 iceberg lettuce, shredded
  oil and vinegar dressing (optional)
  2 cooked chicken breast portions,
    skinned and thinly sliced
  225g/8oz Guacamole
  115g/4oz/1 cup coarsely grated
    Cheddar cheese
  pickled jalapeño chillies, seeded and
    sliced, to taste

1 Heat the oil in a frying pan and fry the tortillas until golden brown on both sides and crisp but not hard.

2 Spread each tortilla with a layer of beans. Put a layer of shredded lettuce (which can be left plain or lightly tossed with a little dressing) over the beans.

3 Arrange pieces of chicken in a layer on top of the lettuce. Carefully spread over a layer of the guacamole and finally, sprinkle over a layer of the grated cheese.

4 Arrange the mixed tostadas on a large platter. Serve on individual plates but eat using your hands.

QUESADILLAS

THESE DELICIOUS FILLED AND DEEP-FRIED TORTILLA TURNOVERS MAKE A POPULAR SNACK AND SMALLER VERSIONS MAKE EXCELLENT CANAPÉS.

MAKES 14

INGREDIENTS
  14 freshly prepared unbaked tortillas

For the filling
  225g/8oz/2 cups finely chopped or
    grated Cheddar cheese
  3 jalapeño chillies, seeded and cut
    into strips
  salt
  oil, for shallow frying

2 Heat the oil in a frying pan, then holding an unbaked tortilla on your palm, put a spoonful of filling along the centre, avoiding the edges.

COOK'S TIP
For other stuffing ideas try leftover beans with chillies, or chopped chorizo sausage fried with a little chopped onion.

3 Fold the tortilla and seal the edges by pressing or crimping well together. Fry in hot oil, on both sides, until golden brown and crisp.

4 Using a metal spatula, lift out the quesadilla and drain it on kitchen paper. Transfer to a plate and keep warm while frying the remaining quesadillas. Serve hot.

1 Have the tortillas ready, covered with a clean cloth. Combine the cheese and chilli strips in a bowl. Season with salt. Set aside.

CHILLIED MONKFISH PARCELS

HOT RED CHILLI, GARLIC AND LEMON RIND ADD TANGY FLAVOUR TO MONKFISH IN THESE TASTY AND APPEALING LITTLE PARCELS.

SERVES 4

INGREDIENTS

175g/6oz/1^{1}/2 cups strong white
  bread flour
2 eggs
115g/4oz skinless monkfish fillet, diced
grated rind of 1 lemon
1 garlic clove, chopped
1 small red chilli, seeded and sliced
45ml/3 tbsp chopped fresh parsley
30ml/2 tbsp single (light) cream

For the tomato oil
2 tomatoes, peeled, seeded and finely diced
45ml/3 tbsp extra virgin olive oil
30ml/1 tbsp fresh lemon juice
salt and ground black pepper

1 Place the flour, eggs and 2.5ml/^{1}/2 tsp salt in a food processor; pulse to form a soft dough. Knead for 2–3 minutes, then wrap in clear film (plastic wrap). Chill for 20 minutes.

2 Place the monkfish, lemon rind, garlic, chilli and parsley in the clean food processor; process until very finely chopped. Add the cream, with plenty of salt and pepper and process again to form a very thick purée.

3 Make the tomato oil by stirring the diced tomato with the olive oil and lemon juice in a bowl. Add salt to taste. Cover and chill.

4 Roll out the dough on a lightly floured surface and cut out 32 rounds, using a 4cm/1^{1}/2in plain cutter. Divide the filling among half the rounds, then cover with the remaining rounds. Pinch the edges tightly to seal, trying to exclude as much air as possible.

5 Bring a large pan of water to simmering point and poach the parcels, in batches, for 2–3 minutes, or until they rise to the surface. Drain and serve hot, drizzled with the tomato oil.

SAMOSAS

A SELECTION OF HIGHLY SPICED VEGETABLES IN A PASTRY CASING MAKES THESE SAMOSAS A DELICIOUS SNACK AT ANY TIME OF THE DAY.

MAKES 30

INGREDIENTS
1 packet spring roll pastry, thawed and
   wrapped in a damp towel
vegetable oil, for deep-frying

For the filling
3 large potatoes, boiled and
   coarsely mashed
75g/3oz/³/₄ cup frozen peas, thawed
50g/2oz/¹/₃ cup canned corn, drained
5ml/1 tsp ground coriander
5ml/1 tsp ground cumin
5ml/1 tsp amchur (dry mango powder)
1 small onion, finely chopped
2 green chillies, finely chopped
30ml/2 tbsp coriander (cilantro)
   leaves, chopped
30ml/2 tbsp mint leaves, chopped
juice of 1 lemon
salt, to taste
chilli sauce, to serve

1 Toss all the filling ingredients together in a large mixing bowl until they are all well blended. Adjust the seasoning with salt and lemon juice, if necessary.

2 Using one strip of pastry at a time, place 15ml/1 tbsp of the filling mixture at one end of the strip and diagonally fold the pastry up to form a triangle shape.

3 Heat enough oil for deep-frying and fry the samosas in small batches until they are golden brown. Keep them hot while frying the rest. Serve hot with chilli sauce.

GUACAMOLE

THIS POPULAR MEXICAN DIP CAN EITHER BE SERVED WITH THE TORTILLA CHIPS OF YOUR CHOICE, OR USED AS A DIP WITH FRESH VEGETABLES.

MAKES 475ML/16FL OZ/2 CUPS

INGREDIENTS
3 large ripe avocados
3 spring onions (scallions), finely chopped
1 garlic clove, crushed
15ml/1 tbsp olive oil
15ml/1 tbsp sour cream
2.5ml/½ tsp salt
30ml/2 tbsp fresh lemon or lime juice
2.5ml/½ tsp cayenne pepper

COOK'S TIP
Guacamole does not keep well, but, if necessary, it can be stored in the refrigerator for a few hours. Cover the surface with clear film (plastic wrap) to prevent discolouring.

1 Halve the avocados and remove the stones (pits). Peel the halves. Put the flesh in a large bowl.

2 With a fork, mash the avocado flesh coarsely.

3 Add the spring onions, garlic, olive oil, cream, salt and lemon or lime juice. Mash until well blended, but do not overwork the mixture. Small chunks of avocado should still remain. Adjust the seasoning, if necessary, with salt or lemon or lime juice. Transfer the mixture to a serving bowl. Serve the dip immediately, sprinkled with the cayenne pepper.

TOMATO SALSA

MAKES 900ML/1½ PINTS/3¾ CUPS

INGREDIENTS
1 fresh hot green chilli, seeded
  and chopped
1 garlic clove
½ red onion, coarsely chopped
3 spring onions (scallions), chopped
15g/½ oz/ ½ cup fresh coriander
  (cilantro) leaves
675g/1½lb ripe tomatoes, seeded and
  coarsely chopped
1–3 canned green chillies
15ml/1 tbsp olive oil
30ml/2 tbsp fresh lime or lemon juice
2.5ml/½ tsp salt, to taste
45ml/3 tbsp tomato juice or cold water

2 Add the tomatoes, canned chillies, olive oil, lime or lemon juice, salt and tomato juice or water. Pulse on and off until chopped; the tomato salsa should be chunky.

3 Transfer to a bowl and taste for seasoning. Leave to stand for at least 30 minutes before serving. This salsa is best served the day it is made.

1 In a food processor or blender, combine the fresh chilli, garlic, chopped red onion, spring onions and coriander leaves. Process until everything is finely chopped.

COOK'S TIP
For less heat, remove the seeds from both fresh and canned chillies.

SEAFOOD WONTONS WITH SPICY DRESSING

THESE TASTY PRAWN AND CRAB MEAT WONTONS ARE SPICED WITH CHILLI AND GINGER, AND SERVED WITH A SPICY SAUCE.

SERVES 4

INGREDIENTS
　225g/8oz raw prawns (shrimp), peeled
　　and deveined
　115g/4oz white crab meat, picked over
　4 canned water chestnuts, finely diced
　1 spring onion (scallion), finely
　　chopped
　1 small green chilli, seeded and
　　finely chopped
　1.25ml/$\frac{1}{2}$ tsp grated fresh root ginger
　20–24 wonton wrappers
　1 egg, separated
　salt and ground black pepper
　coriander (cilantro) leaves, to garnish

For the spicy dressing
　30ml/2 tbsp rice vinegar
　15ml/1 tbsp chopped pickled ginger
　90ml/6 tbsp olive oil
　15ml/1 tbsp soy sauce
　45ml/3 tbsp chopped coriander
　30ml/2 tbsp finely diced red (bell) pepper

1 Finely dice the prawns and place them in a bowl. Add the crab meat, water chestnuts, spring onion, chilli, ginger and egg white. Season with salt and pepper and stir well.

2 Place a wonton wrapper on a board. Put about 5ml/1 tsp of the filling just above the centre of the wrapper. With a pastry brush, moisten the edges of the wrapper with a little of the egg yolk. Bring the bottom of the wrapper up over the filling. Press gently to expel any air, then seal the wrapper neatly in a triangle.

3 For a more elaborate shape, bring the two side points up over the filling, overlap the points and pinch the ends firmly together. Space the filled wontons on a large baking sheet lined with greaseproof (waxed) paper, to prevent them from sticking together.

4 Half fill a large pan with water. Bring to simmering point. Add the filled wontons, a few at a time, and simmer for about 2–3 minutes. The wontons will float to the surface. When ready the wrappers will be translucent and the filling should be cooked. Remove the wontons with a large slotted spoon, drain them briefly, then spread them on trays. Keep warm while cooking the remaining wontons.

5 Make the spicy dressing by whisking all the ingredients together in a bowl. Divide the wontons among serving dishes, drizzle with the dressing and serve garnished with a handful of coriander leaves.

DEVILLED KIDNEYS

"DEVILLED" DISHES ARE ALWAYS HOT AND SPICY. IF YOU HAVE TIME, MIX THE SPICY INGREDIENTS TOGETHER IN ADVANCE TO GIVE THE FLAVOURS TIME TO MINGLE AND MATURE.

SERVES 4

INGREDIENTS

10ml/2 tsp Worcestershire sauce
15ml/1 tbsp prepared English
  (hot) mustard
15ml/1 tbsp lemon juice
15ml/1 tbsp tomato purée (paste)
pinch of cayenne pepper
40g/1¹/₂ oz/3 tbsp butter
1 shallot, finely chopped
8 lamb's kidneys, skinned,
  halved and cored
salt and ground black pepper
15ml/1 tbsp chopped fresh parsley,
  to garnish

1 Mix the Worcestershire sauce, mustard, lemon juice, tomato purée, cayenne pepper and salt together to make a sauce.

2 Melt the butter in a frying pan, add the chopped shallot and cook, stirring occasionally, until it is softened but not coloured.

3 Stir the kidney halves into the shallot in the pan and cook over a medium-high heat for about 3 minutes on each side.

4 Pour the sauce over the kidneys and quickly stir so that they become evenly coated. Serve the dish immediately, sprinkled with chopped fresh parsley.

COOK'S TIP
To remove the cores from the lamb's kidneys, use sharp kitchen scissors, rather than a knife – you will find that it is much easier to do so.

DESERT NACHOS

TORTILLA CHIPS ARE LIVENED UP WITH JALAPEÑOS IN THIS QUICK-AND-EASY SNACK. SERVED WITH A
VARIETY OF SPICY MEXICAN DIPS, THIS ALWAYS PROVES TO BE A POPULAR DISH.

SERVES 2

INGREDIENTS
    450g/1lb blue corn tortilla chips or
      ordinary tortilla chips
    45ml/3 tbsp chopped pickled jalapeño
      chillies, according to taste
    12 black olives, sliced
    225g/8oz/2 cups grated
      Cheddar cheese

To serve
    Guacamole
    Tomato Salsa
    Sour cream

1 Preheat the oven to 180°C/350°F/Gas 4. Put the tortilla chips in a 23 × 33cm/9 × 13in ovenproof dish and spread them out evenly. Sprinkle the jalapeños, olives and cheese evenly over the tortilla chips.

2 Place the prepared tortilla chips in the top of the oven and bake for 10–15 minutes, until the cheese melts. Serve the nachos immediately, with the guacamole, tomato salsa and sour cream for dipping.

HUEVOS RANCHEROS

SERVES 4

INGREDIENTS
    450g/1lb can refried beans
    300ml/¹/₂ pint/1¹/₄ cups enchilada sauce
    oil, for frying
    4 corn tortillas
    4 eggs
    150g/5oz/1¹/₄ cups grated
      Cheddar cheese
    salt and ground black pepper

1 Heat the refried beans in a pan. Cover and set aside.

2 Heat the enchilada sauce in a small pan. Cover and set aside.

COOK'S TIP
For a simple enchilada sauce, blend a can of tomatoes with 3 garlic cloves, 1 chopped onion, 45ml/3 tbsp chilli powder, 5ml/1 tsp each cayenne and cumin, and 2.5ml/¹/₂ tsp each dried oregano and salt.

3 Preheat the oven to 110°C/225°F/ Gas ¹/₄. Put a 5mm/¹/₄in layer of oil in a small non-stick frying pan and heat carefully. When the oil is hot, add the tortillas, one at a time, and fry for about 30 seconds on each side, until just crisp. Remove and drain the tortillas on kitchen paper and keep them warm on a baking sheet in the oven. Discard the oil used for frying. Let the pan cool slightly, then wipe it with kitchen paper to remove all but a film of oil.

4 Heat the frying pan over a low heat. Break in two eggs and cook until the whites are just set. Season with salt and pepper, then transfer to the oven to keep warm. Repeat to cook the remaining eggs.

5 To serve, place a tortilla on each of four plates. Spread a layer of refried beans over each tortilla, then top each with an egg. Spoon over the warm enchilada sauce, then sprinkle with the cheese. Serve hot.

SPICY MEAT-FILLED PARCELS

IN INDONESIA THE FINEST GOSSAMER DOUGH IS MADE FOR MARTABAK. *YOU CAN ACHIEVE EQUALLY GOOD RESULTS USING READY-MADE FILO PASTRY OR SPRING ROLL WRAPPERS.*

MAKES 16

INGREDIENTS
    450g/1lb lean minced beef
    2 small onions, finely chopped
    2 small leeks, very
       finely chopped
    2 garlic cloves, crushed
    10ml/2 tsp coriander seeds, dry-fried
       and ground
    5ml/1 tsp cumin seeds, dry-fried
       and ground
    5–10ml/1–2 tsp mild curry powder
    2 eggs, beaten
    400g/14oz packet filo pastry
    45–60ml/3–4 tbsp sunflower oil
    salt and freshly ground black pepper
    light soy sauce, to serve

1 To make the filling, mix the meat with the onions, leeks, garlic, coriander, cumin, curry powder and seasoning. Turn into a heated wok, without oil, and stir all the time, until the meat has changed colour and looks cooked, about 5 minutes.

2 Allow to cool and then mix in enough beaten egg to bind to a soft consistency. Any leftover egg can be used to seal the edges of the dough; otherwise, use milk.

3 Brush a sheet of filo with oil and lay another sheet on top. Cut the sheets in half. Place a large spoonful of the filling on each double piece of filo. Fold the sides to the middle so that the edges just overlap. Brush these edges with either beaten egg or milk and fold the other two sides to the middle in the same way, so that you now have a square parcel shape. Make sure that the parcel is as flat as possible, to speed cooking. Repeat with the remaining fifteen parcels and place on a floured tray in the fridge.

4 Heat the remaining oil in a shallow pan and cook several parcels at a time, depending on the size of the pan. Cook for 3 minutes on the first side and then turn them over and cook for a further 2 minutes, or until heated through. Cook the remaining parcels in the same way and serve hot, sprinkled with light soy sauce.

5 If preferred, these spicy parcels can be cooked in a hot oven at 200°C/400°F/ Gas 6 for 20 minutes. Glaze with more beaten egg before baking for a rich, golden colour.

WELSH RABBIT

This delicious supper dish is made from toast and a flavourful cheese sauce spiked with hot mustard and Worcestershire sauce. It doesn't, as the name might suggest, contain any meat. It is also called "Welsh Rarebit", although "rabbit" seems to have been the original name.

SERVES 4

INGREDIENTS

4 thick slices of bread, crusts removed
25g/1oz/2 tbsp butter
225g/8oz/2 cups grated mature (sharp)
  Cheddar cheese
5ml/1 tsp English (hot) mustard
  powder
few drops Worcestershire sauce
60ml/4 tbsp brown ale, beer or milk

COOK'S TIP
Use a strong-tasting cheese so the
topping has plenty of flavour.

1 Preheat the grill (broiler). Toast the
bread until golden, then place in a single
layer in a wide, shallow ovenproof dish.
Keep warm.

2 Slowly melt the butter in a small to
medium, heavy, preferably non-stick pan
over a very low heat, or in a bowl placed
over a pan of hot water. Stir it constantly
as it melts, then remove from the heat.

3 Stir the cheese, mustard powder and
Worcestershire sauce into the butter, then
slowly pour in the ale, beer or milk in a
steady stream, stirring the cheese mixture
constantly until very well blended.

4 Preheat the grill. Spoon the Cheddar
cheese mixture on to the toast in the
ovenproof dish, then place it under the
hot grill until it is bubbling hot and golden
brown in colour. Serve immediately.

CHICKEN NAAN POCKETS

THIS QUICK-AND-EASY DISH IS IDEAL FOR A SNACK LUNCH OR SUPPER.

SERVES 4

INGREDIENTS
4 naan
45ml/3 tbsp natural (plain) yogurt
7.5ml/1$\frac{1}{2}$ tsp garam masala
5ml/1 tsp chilli powder
5ml/1 tsp salt
45ml/3 tbsp lemon juice
15ml/1 tbsp chopped fresh coriander
 (cilantro)
1 fresh green chilli, chopped
450g/1lb chicken, skinned, boned
 and cubed
15ml/1 tbsp vegetable oil
8 onion rings
2 tomatoes, quartered
$\frac{1}{2}$ white cabbage, shredded
lemon wedges, 2 small tomatoes,
 halved, mixed salad leaves and fresh
 coriander, to garnish

1 Using a small, sharp knife, carefully cut into the middle of each naan to make a pocket, then set them aside until needed.

2 In a bowl, mix together the natural yogurt, garam masala, chilli powder, salt, lemon juice, fresh coriander and chopped fresh green chilli. Pour this marinade over the chicken pieces and leave to marinate for about 1 hour.

3 After 1 hour preheat the grill (broiler) to very hot, then lower the heat to medium. Place the marinated chicken pieces in a flameproof dish and grill (broil) for about 15–20 minutes, until they are tender and cooked through, turning the chicken pieces at least twice. Baste with the vegetable oil occasionally while cooking.

4 Remove the dish from the heat and fill each naan with the chicken and then with the onion rings, tomatoes and shredded cabbage. Serve garnished with lemon, tomatoes, salad leaves and coriander.

CHICKEN TIKKA

A MIXTURE OF GINGER, GARLIC AND CHILLI POWDER ADDS A CHARACTERISTIC SPICY TASTE TO THIS POPULAR INDIAN APPETIZER WHICH IS QUICK AND EASY TO COOK.

SERVES 6

INGREDIENTS
450g/1lb chicken, skinned, boned
 and cubed
5ml/1 tsp ginger pulp
5ml/1 tsp garlic pulp
5ml/1 tsp chilli powder
1.5ml/$\frac{1}{4}$ tsp ground turmeric
5ml/1 tsp salt
150ml/$\frac{1}{4}$ pint/$\frac{2}{3}$ cup natural
 (plain) yogurt
60ml/4 tbsp lemon juice
15ml/1 tbsp chopped fresh
 coriander (cilantro)
15ml/1 tbsp vegetable oil
1 small onion, cut into rings, lime
 wedges, mixed salad and fresh
 coriander, to garnish

1 In a medium mixing bowl, combine the chicken pieces, ginger and garlic pulp, chilli powder, turmeric, salt, yogurt, lemon juice and fresh coriander and leave to marinate for at least 2 hours.

2 Place the marinated chicken on a grill (broiler) tray or in a flameproof dish lined with foil and baste with the vegetable oil.

3 Preheat the grill to medium. Grill (broil) the chicken for 15–20 minutes, until cooked, turning and basting 2–3 times. Serve garnished with onion, lime, salad and coriander.

COOK'S TIP
Chicken tikka can be served with naan or chapatis, pickles and salad as a main dish for four people.

SPICY KEBABS

MAKES 18–20 BALLS

INGREDIENTS
  450g/1lb minced (ground) beef
  1 egg
  3 garlic cloves, crushed
  1/2 onion, finely chopped
  2.5ml/1/2 tsp ground black
    pepper
  7.5ml/11/2 tsp ground cumin
  7.5ml/11/2 tsp ground coriander
  5ml/1 tsp ground ginger
  10ml/2 tsp garam masala
  15ml/1 tbsp lemon juice
  50–75g/2–3oz/1–11/2 cups fresh white
    breadcrumbs
  1 small chilli, seeded and chopped
  salt
  oil, for deep-frying

1 Place the minced beef in a large bowl and add the egg, garlic, onion, spices, seasoning, lemon juice, about 50g/1oz/1/2 cup of the breadcrumbs and the chilli.

2 Using your hands or a wooden spoon, mix the ingredients together until the mixture is firm. If it feels sticky, add more of the breadcrumbs and mix again until firm.

3 Heat the oil in a large heavy pan or deep-fat fryer. Shape the mixture into balls or fingers and fry, a few at a time, for 5 minutes or until well browned all over.

4 Using a slotted spoon, drain the kebabs and then transfer to a plate lined with kitchen paper. Cook the remaining kebabs in the same way and then serve, if you like, with Kachumbali or a spicy dip.

COD WITH CHILLI AND MUSTARD SEEDS

SERVES 4

INGREDIENTS

30ml/2 tbsp olive oil
5ml/1 tsp mustard seeds
1 large potato, cubed
2 slices of Serrano ham, shredded
1 onion, thinly sliced
2 garlic cloves, thinly sliced
1 red chilli, seeded and sliced
115g/4oz skinless, boneless cod, cubed
120ml/4fl oz/^{1}/$_2$ cup vegetable stock
50g/2oz/^{1}/$_2$ cup grated tasty cheese,
  such as Manchego or Cheddar
salt and ground black pepper

COOK'S TIP
If you prefer a crisp topping, replace
half the cheese with wholemeal
(whole-wheat) breadcrumbs.

1 Heat the oil in a heavy frying pan. Add
the mustard seeds. Cook for 1–2 minutes,
until the seeds begin to pop and splutter,
then add the potato, ham and onion.

2 Cook, stirring regularly for about
10–15 minutes, until the potatoes are
brown and almost tender.

3 Add the garlic and chilli and cook for
2 minutes more.

4 Stir in the cod cubes and cook for
2–3 minutes, until white, then add the
stock and plenty of salt and pepper.
Cover the pan and cook for 5 minutes,
until the fish is just cooked and the
potatoes are tender.

5 Transfer the mixture to a flame-proof
dish. Sprinkle over the grated cheese and
place under a hot grill (broiler) for about
2–3 minutes, until the cheese is golden
and bubbling.

FRIED DOUGH BALLS WITH FIERY SALSA

THESE CRUNCHY DOUGH BALLS ARE ACCOMPANIED BY A HOT AND SPICY TOMATO SALSA. SERVE THEM WITH A JUICY TOMATO SALAD, IF YOU PREFER.

SERVES 10

INGREDIENTS
    450g/1lb/4 cups strong white
      bread flour
    5ml/1 tsp easy-blend (rapid-rise)
      dried yeast
    5ml/1 tsp salt
    30ml/2 tbsp chopped fresh parsley
    2 garlic cloves, finely chopped
    30ml/2 tbsp olive oil, plus extra
      for greasing
    vegetable oil, for frying

For the salsa
    6 hot red chillies, seeded and
      coarsely chopped
    1 onion, coarsely chopped
    2 garlic cloves, quartered
    2.5cm/1in piece of root ginger,
      coarsely chopped
    450g/1lb tomatoes, coarsely chopped
    30ml/2 tbsp olive oil
    pinch of sugar
    salt and ground black pepper

2 Gather the dough in the bowl together, then tip it out on to a lightly floured surface or board. Knead for about 10 minutes, until the dough feels very smooth and elastic.

3 Rub a little oil into the surface of the dough. Return it to the clean bowl, cover it with clear film (plastic wrap) or a clean dishtowel and leave in a warm place to rise for about 1 hour, or until it has doubled in bulk.

4 Meanwhile, make the salsa. Combine the chillies, onion, garlic and ginger in a food processor and process together until very finely chopped. Add the tomatoes and olive oil and process until smooth.

5 Sieve the mixture into a pan. Add sugar, salt and pepper to taste and simmer gently for 15 minutes. Do not allow the salsa to boil.

6 Roll the dough into about 40 balls. Shallow fry in batches in hot oil for 4–5 minutes, until crisp and golden. Drain on kitchen paper and serve hot, with the fiery salsa in a separate bowl for dipping.

1 Sift the flour into a large bowl. Stir in the yeast and salt and make a well in the centre. Add the chopped parsley, garlic, olive oil and enough warm water to make a firm dough.

COOK'S TIP
These dough balls can be deep-fried for about 3–4 minutes or baked at 200°C/400°F/ Gas 6 for approximately 15–20 minutes.

CHEESE FRITTERS

THESE CRISP FRITTERS OWE THEIR INSPIRATION TO ITALY. A NOTE OF CAUTION — DO BE CAREFUL NOT TO BURN YOUR MOUTH WHEN YOU TAKE YOUR FIRST BITE, AS THE SOFT, RICH CHEESE FILLING WILL BE VERY HOT.

MAKES 15–16

INGREDIENTS
115g/4oz/^{1}/$_2$ cup ricotta cheese
50g/2oz/^{1}/$_3$ cup finely grated
   fontina cheese
25g/1oz/^{1}/$_2$ cup grated Parmesan cheese
2.5ml/^{1}/$_2$ tsp cayenne pepper
1 egg, beaten, plus a little extra to
   seal the wontons
15–16 wonton wrappers
oil for deep-frying

1 Line a large baking sheet with greaseproof (waxed) paper or sprinkle it with flour. Set aside. Combine the cheeses in a bowl, then add the cayenne and beaten egg and mix well.

2 Place one wonton wrapper at a time on a board. Brush the edges with egg. Spoon a little filling in the centre; pull the top corner down to the bottom corner, to make a triangle.

3 Transfer the filled wontons to the prepared baking sheet.

4 Heat the oil in a deep-fryer or large pan. Slip in as many wontons at one time as can be accommodated without overcrowding. Fry them for 2–3 minutes on each side, or until the fritters are golden. Remove with a slotted spoon. Drain on kitchen paper and serve immediately.

CHILLED SOBA NOODLES WITH NORI

SERVES 4

INGREDIENTS
350g/12oz dried soba noodles
1 sheet nori seaweed

For the dipping sauce
300ml/^{1}/$_2$ pint/1^1/$_4$ cups fish stock
120ml/4fl oz/^{1}/$_2$ cup dark soy sauce
60ml/4 tbsp mirin
5ml/1 tsp sugar
15ml/1 tbsp fish sauce

Flavourings
4 spring onions (scallions), finely chopped
30ml/2 tbsp grated mooli (daikon)
wasabi paste
4 egg yolks (optional)

COOK'S TIP
Mooli is a slim white vegetable, sometimes also known as daikon.

1 Make the dipping sauce. Combine the stock, soy sauce, mirin and sugar in a pan. Bring rapidly to the boil, add the fish sauce, then remove from the heat. When cool, strain the sauce into a bowl and cover. This can be done in advance and the sauce kept chilled for up to a week.

2 Cook the soba noodles in a pan of lightly salted, boiling water for 6–7 minutes, or until just tender, following the manufacturer's instructions on the packet.

3 Drain and rinse the noodles under cold running water, agitating them gently to remove the excess starch. Drain well.

4 Toast the nori over a high gas flame or under a hot grill (broiler), then crumble them into thin strips. Divide the noodles among four serving dishes and top with the nori. Serve each portion with an individual bowl of dipping sauce and offer the flavourings separately.

Fresh fish is popular all over the world and there are hundreds of ways of adding spicy flavour; fish can be fired up with hot red chillies or chilli paste, pickled with jalapeño chillies or made into a curry with aromatic warm spices and spiked with hot chilli powder. Steamed Fish with Chilli Sauce is a delicious dish — the fish is cooked to perfection, with all the moistness and flavour retained.

Fiery Fish
and Shellfish

STEAMED FISH WITH CHILLI SAUCE

IN THIS RED-HOT DISH FROM THAILAND, WHOLE FISH IS COOKED WITH RED CHILLIES, GINGER AND LEMON GRASS, THEN SERVED WITH A MOUTH-TINGLING CHILLI SAUCE.

SERVES 4

INGREDIENTS

    1 large or 2 medium firm fish like bass
       or grouper, scaled and cleaned
    1 fresh banana leaf
    30ml/2 tbsp rice wine
    3 red chillies, seeded and finely sliced
    2 garlic cloves, finely chopped
    2cm/³/4 in piece fresh root ginger,
       finely shredded
    2 lemon grass stalks, crushed
       and finely chopped
    2 spring onions (scallions), chopped
    30ml/2 tbsp fish sauce
    juice of 1 lime

For the chilli sauce
    10 red chillies, seeded and chopped
    4 garlic cloves, chopped
    60 ml/4 tbsp fish sauce
    15ml/1 tbsp sugar
    75ml/5 tbsp lime juice

1 Rinse the fish under cold running water. Pat dry with kitchen paper. With a sharp knife, slash the skin of the fish a few times on both sides.

2 Place the fish on a banana leaf. Mix together all the remaining ingredients and spread over the fish.

3 Place a small upturned plate in the base of a wok and add 5cm/2in boiling water; place a banana leaf on top. Lift the banana leaf, together with the fish, and place on the plate or rack. Cover with a lid and steam for 10–15 minutes, or until the fish is cooked.

4 Place all the chilli sauce ingredients in a food processor and process until smooth. You may need to add a little cold water if the mixture is too thick.

5 Serve the fish hot, on the banana leaf if you like, with the sweet chilli sauce to spoon over the top.

FRIED CATFISH FILLETS WITH PIQUANT SAUCE

SPICY FILLETS OF CATFISH ARE FRIED IN A HERBED BATTER AND SERVED WITH A WONDERFULLY TASTY SAUCE
TO CREATE THIS EXCELLENT SUPPER DISH.

SERVES 4

INGREDIENTS

1 egg
50ml/2fl oz/^{1}/$_4$ cup olive oil
squeeze of lemon juice
2.5ml/^{1}/$_2$ tsp chopped fresh dill
4 catfish fillets
50g/2oz/^{1}/$_2$ cup flour
25g/1 oz/2 tbsp butter or margarine
salt and ground black pepper

For the sauce

1 egg yolk
30ml/2 tbsp Dijon mustard
30ml/2 tbsp white wine vinegar
10ml/2 tsp paprika
300ml/^{1}/$_2$ pint/1^1/$_4$ cups olive or
   vegetable oil
30ml/2 tbsp prepared horseradish
2.5ml/^{1}/$_2$ tsp chopped garlic
1 celery stick, chopped
30ml/2 tbsp tomato ketchup
2.5ml/^{1}/$_2$ tsp ground black pepper
2.5ml/^{1}/$_2$ tsp salt

1 For the sauce, combine the egg yolk mustard, vinegar and paprika in a mixing bowl. Add the oil in a thin stream, beating vigorously with a wire whisk to blend it in.

2 When the mixture is smooth and thick, beat in all the other sauce ingredients. Cover and chill until ready to serve.

3 Combine the egg, 15ml/1 tbsp olive oil, the lemon juice, dill and a little salt and pepper in a shallow dish. Beat until well combined.

4 Dip both sides of each catfish fillet in the egg and herb mixture, then coat lightly with flour, shaking off any excess from it.

5 Heat the butter or margarine with the remaining olive oil in a large, heavy frying pan. Add the fish fillets and fry until they are golden brown on both sides and cooked, about 8–10 minutes. To test they are done, insert the point of a sharp knife into the fish: the flesh should be opaque in the centre.

6 Serve the fried catfish fillets hot, accompanied by the piquant sauce.

COOK'S TIP
If you can't find catfish, use any firm fish fillets instead. Cod or haddock fillets both make good substitutes.

PICKLED FISH

<u>SERVES 4</u>

INGREDIENTS
  900g/2lb white fish fillets
  60ml/4 tbsp freshly squeezed lime or
    lemon juice
  300ml/½ pint/1¼ cups olive or corn oil
  2 whole cloves
  6 peppercorns
  2 garlic cloves
  2.5ml/½ tsp ground cumin
  2.5ml/½ tsp dried oregano
  2 bay leaves
  1 drained canned jalapeño chilli,
    seeded, and cut into strips
  1 onion, thinly sliced
  250ml/8fl oz/1 cup white wine vinegar
  250ml/8fl oz/1 cup olive or corn oil
  salt

For the garnish
  lettuce leaves
  green olives

1 Cut the fish fillets into eight pieces and arrange them in a single layer in a shallow dish. Drizzle with the lime or lemon juice. Cover and marinate for 15 minutes, turning the fillets once.

2 Lift out the fillets with a spatula, pat them dry with kitchen paper and season with salt. Heat 60ml/4 tbsp of the oil in a frying pan and sauté the fish until lightly golden brown. Transfer to a platter and set aside.

3 Combine the cloves, peppercorns, garlic, cumin, oregano, bay leaves, chilli and vinegar in a pan. Bring to the boil, then simmer for 3–4 minutes.

4 Add the remaining oil, and bring to a simmer. Pour over the fish. Allow to cool, then cover and chill for 24 hours. To serve, lift out the fillets with a spatula and arrange on a serving dish. Garnish with lettuce and olives.

COOK'S TIP
To make the dish special, add an elaborate garnish of radishes, capers and chilli strips.

RED SNAPPER, VERACRUZ-STYLE

THIS IS MEXICO'S BEST-KNOWN FISH DISH. IN VERACRUZ RED SNAPPER IS ALWAYS USED BUT FILLETS OF ANY FIRM-FLESHED WHITE FISH CAN BE SUBSTITUTED SUCCESSFULLY.

SERVES 4

INGREDIENTS

4 large red snapper fillets
30ml/2 tbsp freshly squeezed lime or
   lemon juice
120ml/4fl oz/^{1}/$_{2}$ cup olive oil
1 onion, finely chopped
2 garlic cloves, chopped
675g/1^{1}/$_{2}$ lb tomatoes, peeled
   and chopped
1 bay leaf, plus a few sprigs to garnish
1.5ml/^{1}/$_{4}$ tsp dried oregano
30ml/2 tbsp large capers, plus extra
   to serve (optional)
16 pitted green olives, halved
2 drained canned jalapeño chillies,
   seeded and cut into strips
butter, for frying
3 slices firm white bread, cut
   into triangles
salt and ground black pepper

1 Arrange the fish fillets in a single layer in a shallow dish. Season with salt and pepper, drizzle with the lime or lemon juice and set aside.

2 Heat the oil in a large frying pan and sauté the onion and garlic until the onion is soft. Add the tomatoes and cook for about 10 minutes, until the mixture is thick, stirring occasionally.

3 Stir in the bay leaf, oregano, capers, olives and chillies. Add the fish and cook over a very low heat for about 10 minutes, or until tender.

COOK'S TIP
This dish can also be made with a whole fish, weighing about 1.5kg/3–3½lb. Bake together with the sauce, in a preheated oven at 160°C/325°F/Gas 3. Allow 10 minutes cooking time for every 2.5cm/1in thickness of the fish.

4 While the fish is cooking, heat the butter in a small frying pan and sauté the bread triangles until they are golden brown on both sides.

5 Transfer the fish to a warm platter, pour over the sauce and surround with the fried bread triangles. Garnish with bay leaves and serve with extra capers, if you like.

PRAWNS WITH CHAYOTE IN TURMERIC SAUCE

GALANGAL, RED CHILLIES AND TURMERIC ADD DISTINCTIVE HOT AND SPICY FLAVOURS TO THIS TASTY INDONESIAN DISH.

SERVES 4

INGREDIENTS

1–2 chayotes or 2–3 courgettes (zucchini)
2 fresh red chillies, seeded
1 onion, quartered
5mm/$\frac{1}{4}$ in fresh galangal, peeled
1 lemon grass stalk, lower 5cm/2in
  sliced, top bruised
2.5cm/1in fresh turmeric, peeled
200ml/7fl oz/scant 1 cup water
lemon juice
400ml/14fl oz can coconut milk
450g/1 lb cooked peeled prawns (shrimp)
salt
red chilli shreds, to garnish (optional)
boiled rice, to serve

1 Peel the chayotes, remove the seeds and cut into strips. If using courgettes, cut into 5cm/2in strips.

2 Grind the fresh red chillies, onion, sliced galangal, sliced lemon grass and the fresh turmeric to a paste in a food processor or with a mortar and pestle. Add the water to the paste mixture, with a squeeze of lemon juice and salt to taste.

3 Pour into a pan. Add the top of the lemon grass stalk. Bring to the boil and cook for 1–2 minutes. Add the chayote or courgette pieces and cook for 2 minutes. Stir in the coconut milk. Taste and adjust the seasoning.

4 Stir in the prawns and cook gently for 2–3 minutes. Remove the lemon grass stalk. Garnish with shreds of chilli, if using, and serve with rice.

INDONESIAN SPICY FISH

FISH IS GIVEN A HOT, PIQUANT TWIST IN THIS FLAVOURFUL DISH.

SERVES 6–8

INGREDIENTS

1 kg/2$\frac{1}{4}$ lb fresh mackerel
  fillets, skinned
30ml/2 tbsp tamarind pulp, soaked in
  200ml/7fl oz/scant 1 cup water
1 onion
1cm/$\frac{1}{2}$ in fresh galangal, peeled
2 garlic cloves
1–2 fresh red chillies, seeded, or 5ml/
  1 tsp chilli powder
5ml/1 tsp ground coriander
5ml/1 tsp ground turmeric
2.5ml/$\frac{1}{2}$ tsp ground fennel seeds
15ml/1 tbsp dark brown sugar
90–105ml/6–7 tbsp oil
200ml/7fl oz/scant 1 cup
  coconut cream
salt and ground black pepper
fresh chilli shreds, to garnish

1 Rinse the fish fillets in cold water and dry them well on kitchen paper. Put into a shallow dish and sprinkle with a little salt. Strain the tamarind and pour the juice over the fish fillets. Leave for 30 minutes.

2 Quarter the onion, peel and slice the galangal and peel the garlic. Grind the onion, galangal, garlic and chillies or chilli powder to a paste in a food processor or with a mortar and pestle. Add the ground coriander, turmeric, fennel seeds and brown sugar.

3 Heat half of the oil in a frying pan. Drain the fish fillets and cook for 5 minutes, or until tender. Set aside.

4 Wipe out the pan and heat the remaining oil. Fry the spice paste, stirring constantly, until it gives off a spicy aroma. Do not let it brown. Add the coconut cream and simmer gently for a few minutes. Add the fish fillets and gently heat through.

5 Taste for seasoning and serve sprinkled with shredded chilli.

BRAISED FISH IN CHILLI AND GARLIC SAUCE

SERVES 4–6

INGREDIENTS

   1 bream or trout, 675g/1¹/2 lb, cleaned
   15ml/1 tbsp light soy sauce
   15ml/1 tbsp Chinese rice wine
   vegetable oil, for deep-frying

For the sauce
   2 garlic cloves, finely chopped
   2–3 spring onions (scallions),
     finely chopped
   5ml/1 tsp chopped fresh root ginger
   30ml/2 tbsp chilli bean sauce
   15ml/1 tbsp tomato purée (paste)
   10ml/2 tsp light brown sugar
   15ml/1 tbsp rice vinegar
   about 120ml/4fl oz/¹/2 cup fish stock
   15ml/1 tbsp cornflour (cornstarch)
     paste
   few drops sesame oil

1 Rinse and dry the fish well. Using a sharp knife, score both sides of the fish as far down as the bone with diagonal cuts about 2.5cm/1in apart. Rub the whole fish with soy sauce and wine on both sides, then leave to marinate for 10–15 minutes.

2 In a wok, deep-fry the fish in hot oil for about 3–4 minutes on both sides until golden brown.

3 Pour off the excess oil, leaving a thin layer in the wok. Push the fish to one side of the wok and add the garlic, the white part of the spring onions, fresh ginger, chilli bean sauce, tomato purée, brown sugar, rice vinegar and stock. Bring to the boil and braise the fish in the sauce for about 4–5 minutes, turning it over once. Add the green part of the chopped spring onions. Thicken the sauce with the cornflour paste, sprinkle with the sesame oil and place on a dish to serve immediately.

VARIATION
Any whole fish is suitable for this dish; try sea bass, grouper or grey mullet, if you like. Also, if you can't find Chinese wine, you can use dry sherry instead.

SALT COD IN MILD CHILLI SAUCE

SERVES 6

INGREDIENTS
   900g/2lb dried salt cod
   1 onion, chopped
   2 garlic cloves, chopped

For the sauce
   6 dried ancho chillies
   1 onion, chopped
   2.5ml/$\frac{1}{2}$ tsp dried oregano
   2.5ml/$\frac{1}{2}$ tsp ground coriander
   1 serrano chilli, seeded and chopped
   45ml/3 tbsp corn oil
   750ml/1$\frac{1}{4}$ pints/3 cups fish or
      chicken stock
   salt

For the garnish
   1 fresh green chilli, sliced

COOK'S TIP
Dried salt cod is a great favourite in
Spain and Portugal and throughout
Latin America. Look for it in Spanish
and Portuguese markets.

1 Soak the cod in cold water for several hours, depending on how hard and salty it is. Change the water once or twice during soaking.

2 Drain the fish and transfer it to a pan. Pour in water to cover. Bring to a gentle simmer and cook for about 15 minutes, until the fish is tender. Drain, reserving the stock. Remove any skin or bones from the fish and cut it into 4cm/1$\frac{1}{2}$ in pieces.

3 Make the sauce. Remove the stems and shake the seeds from the ancho chillies. Tear the pods into pieces, put in a bowl of warm water and soak until they are soft.

4 Drain the soaked chillies and put them into a food processor with the onion, oregano, coriander and serrano chilli. Process to a purée.

5 Heat the oil in a frying pan and cook the purée, stirring, for about 5 minutes. Stir in the fish or chicken stock and simmer for 3–4 minutes.

6 Add the prepared cod and simmer for a few minutes longer to heat the fish through and blend the flavours. Serve garnished with the sliced chilli.

BAKED OR GRILLED SPICED WHOLE FISH

<u>SERVES 6</u>

INGREDIENTS

1 kg/2¹/₄ lb bream, carp or pomfret,
  cleaned and scaled if necessary
1 fresh red chilli, seeded and ground,
  or 5ml/1 tsp chopped chilli
  from a jar
4 garlic cloves, crushed
2.5cm/1 in fresh root ginger, peeled
  and sliced
4 spring onions (scallions), chopped
juice of ¹/₂ lemon
30ml/2 tbsp sunflower oil
salt

1 Rinse the fish and dry it well inside and out with absorbent kitchen paper. Slash two or three times through the fleshy part on each side of the fish.

2 Place the chilli, garlic, ginger and spring onions in a food processor and blend to a paste, or grind the mixture together with a mortar and pestle. Add the lemon juice and salt, then stir in the oil.

3 Spoon a little of the mixture inside the fish and pour the rest over the top. Turn the fish to coat it completely in the spice mixture and leave to marinate for at least 1 hour.

4 Preheat the grill (broiler). Place a long strip of double foil under the fish to support it and to make turning it over easier. Put on a rack in a grill pan and cook under the hot grill for 5 minutes on one side and 8 minutes on the second side, basting with the marinade during cooking. Serve with boiled rice.

VINEGAR CHILLI FISH

<u>SERVES 2–3</u>

INGREDIENTS

2–3 mackerel, filleted
2–3 fresh red chillies, seeded
4 macadamia nuts or 8 almonds
1 red onion, quartered
2 garlic cloves, crushed
1 cm/¹/₂ in fresh root ginger, peeled
  and sliced
5ml/1 tsp ground turmeric
45ml/3 tbsp coconut or vegetable oil
45ml/3 tbsp wine vinegar
150ml/¹/₄ pint/²/₃ cup water
salt
deep-fried onions, to garnish
finely chopped fresh chilli, to garnish

1 Rinse the fish fillets in cold water and then dry them well on kitchen paper. Set aside.

2 Grind the chillies, nuts, onion, garlic, ginger, turmeric and 15ml/1 tbsp of the oil to a paste in a food processor or with a mortar and pestle. Heat the remaining oil in a frying pan and cook the paste for 1–2 minutes, without browning. Stir in the vinegar and water. Add salt to taste. Bring to the boil, then reduce to a simmer.

3 Place the fish fillets in the sauce. Cover and cook for 6–8 minutes, or until the fish is tender.

4 Lift the fish on to a plate and keep warm. Reduce the sauce by boiling rapidly for 1 minute. Pour over the fish and serve. Garnish with deep-fried onions and chopped chilli.

MEXICAN SPICY FISH

This is a typical Mexican dish.

SERVES 6

INGREDIENTS
    1.5kg/3 – 3¹/₂ lb striped bass or any
        non-oily white fish, cut into 6 steaks
    120ml/4fl oz/¹/₂ cup corn oil
    1 large onion, thinly sliced
    2 garlic cloves, chopped
    350g/12oz tomatoes, sliced
    2 drained canned jalapeño chillies,
        rinsed and sliced

For the marinade
    4 garlic cloves, crushed
    5ml/1 tsp black peppercorns
    5ml/1 tsp dried oregano
    2.5ml/¹/₂ tsp ground cumin
    5ml/1 tsp ground annatto
    2.5ml/¹/₂ tsp ground cinnamon
    120ml/4fl oz/¹/₂ cup mild white vinegar
    salt
    flat leaf parsley, to garnish

1 Arrange the fish steaks in a single layer in a shallow dish. Make the marinade. Using a pestle, grind the garlic and black peppercorns in a mortar. Add the dried oregano, cumin, annatto and cinnamon and mix to a paste with the vinegar. Add salt to taste and spread the marinade on both sides of each of the fish steaks. Cover and leave in a cool place for 1 hour.

2 Select a flameproof dish large enough to hold the fish in a single layer and pour in enough of the oil to coat the base. Arrange the fish in the dish with any remaining marinade.

3 Top the fish with the onion, garlic, tomatoes and chillies and pour the rest of the oil over the top.

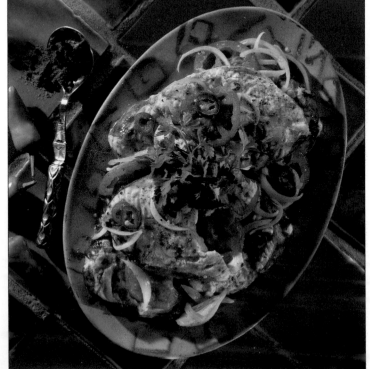

4 Cover the dish and cook over a low heat on top of the stove for 15–20 minutes, or until the fish is no longer translucent. Serve immediately, garnished with the flat leaf parsley.

CITRUS FISH WITH CHILLIES

SERVES 4

INGREDIENTS

4 halibut or cod steaks, 175g/6oz each
juice of 1 lemon
5ml/1 tsp garlic granules
5ml/1 tsp paprika
5ml/1 tsp ground cumin
4ml/^{3}/$_4$ tsp dried tarragon
about 60ml/4 tbsp olive oil
flour, for dusting
300ml/^{1}/$_2$ pint/1^1/$_4$ cups fish stock
2 red chillies, seeded and
    finely chopped
30ml/2 tbsp chopped fresh
    coriander (cilantro)
1 red onion, cut into rings
salt and ground black pepper

1 Place the fish in a shallow bowl and mix together the lemon juice, garlic, paprika, cumin, tarragon and a little salt and pepper. Spoon over the lemon mixture, cover loosely with clear film (plastic wrap) and marinate for a few hours or overnight in the refrigerator.

2 Gently heat all of the oil in a large non-stick frying pan, dust the fish with flour and then fry the fish for a few minutes each side, until golden brown all over.

3 Pour the fish stock around the fish, and simmer, covered for about 5 minutes, until the fish is thoroughly cooked through.

4 Add the chopped red chillies and 15ml/1 tbsp of the coriander to the pan. Simmer for 5 minutes.

5 Transfer the fish and sauce to a serving plate and keep warm.

6 Wipe the pan, heat some olive oil and stir-fry the onion rings until speckled brown. Sprinkle over the fish with the remaining chopped coriander and serve immediately.

SAFFRON FISH

SERVES 4

INGREDIENTS

2–3 saffron threads
2 egg yolks
1 garlic clove, crushed
4 salmon trout steaks
oil for deep-frying
salt and ground black pepper
green salad, to serve

1 Soak the saffron in 15ml/1 tbsp boiling water and then beat the mixture into the egg yolks. Season to taste with garlic, salt and pepper.

COOK'S TIP
Any type of fish can be used in this recipe. Try a combination of plain and smoked, such as smoked and unsmoked cod or haddock.

2 Place the fish steaks in a shallow dish and coat with the egg mixture. Cover with clear film (plastic wrap) and marinate for up to 1 hour.

3 Heat the oil in a deep-fryer until it is very hot, then fry the fish, one steak at a time, for about 10 minutes, until golden brown. Drain each steak on kitchen paper. Serve with a green salad.

PAN-FRIED SPICY SARDINES

THIS DELICIOUS FISH RECIPE IS A FAVOURITE IN MANY ARAB COUNTRIES.

SERVES 4

INGREDIENTS

10g/¼ oz fresh parsley
3–4 garlic cloves, crushed
8–12 sardines, prepared
30ml/2 tbsp lemon juice
50g/2oz/½ cup plain (all-purpose) flour
2.5ml/½ tsp ground cumin
60ml/4 tbsp vegetable oil
salt and ground black pepper
naan bread and salad, to serve

COOK'S TIP
If you don't have a garlic crusher, crush the garlic using the flat side of a large knife blade instead.

1 Finely chop the parsley and mix in a small bowl with the garlic.

2 Pat the parsley and garlic mixture all over the outsides and insides of the sardines. Sprinkle them with the lemon juice and set aside, covered, in a cool place for about 2 hours to absorb all the flavours.

3 Place the flour on a large plate and season with cumin, salt and pepper. Roll the sardines in the flour, taking care to coat each fish throughly.

4 Heat the oil in a large frying pan and fry the fish, in batches, for 5 minutes on each side, until crisp. Keep warm in the oven while cooking the remaining fish and then serve with naan bread and salad.

WHOLE FISH WITH SWEET AND SOUR SAUCE

SERVES 4

INGREDIENTS
1 whole fish, such as red snapper or
   carp, about 1kg/2^1/4 lb
30–45ml/2–3 tbsp cornflour
   (cornstarch)
oil, for frying
salt and ground black pepper
boiled rice, to serve

For the spice paste
2 garlic cloves
2 lemon grass stalks
2.5cm/1in fresh galangal, peeled
2.5cm/1in fresh root ginger
2cm/^{3}/4 in fresh turmeric or 2.5ml/
   ^{1}/2 tsp ground turmeric
5 macadamia nuts or 10 almonds

For the sauce
15ml/1 tbsp brown sugar
45ml/3 tbsp cider vinegar
about 350ml/12fl oz/1^1/2 cups water
2 lime leaves, torn
4 shallots, quartered
3 tomatoes, peeled and cut in wedges
3 spring onions (scallions), shredded
1 fresh red chilli, seeded and shredded

1 Ask the fishmonger to clean and scale the fish, leaving on the head and tail, or you may do this yourself. Wash and dry the fish thoroughly and then sprinkle it inside and out with salt. Set aside for 15 minutes, while preparing the other ingredients.

2 Peel and crush the garlic cloves. Use only the lower white part of the lemon grass stalks and slice thinly. Peel and slice the fresh galangal, the fresh root ginger and fresh turmeric and grind to a fine paste in a food processor or with a mortar and pestle.

3 Scrape the paste into a bowl. Stir in the brown sugar, cider vinegar, seasoning to taste and the water. Add the lime leaves.

4 Dust the fish with the cornflour and fry on both sides in hot oil for about 8–9 minutes, or until almost cooked through. Drain the fish on kitchen paper and transfer to a serving dish. Keep warm.

5 Pour off most of the oil and then pour in the spicy liquid and bring to the boil. Reduce the heat and cook for about 3–4 minutes. Add the shallots and tomatoes, followed a minute later by the spring onions and chilli. Taste and adjust the seasoning.

6 Pour the sauce over the fish. Serve immediately, with plenty of rice.

TURKISH COLD FISH

GREEN CHILLI, GARLIC AND PAPRIKA ADD SUBTLE SPICING TO THIS DELICIOUS FISH DISH. COLD FISH IS ENJOYED IN MANY PARTS OF THE MIDDLE EAST — THIS PARTICULAR VERSION IS FROM TURKEY.

SERVES 4

INGREDIENTS

60ml/4 tbsp olive oil
900g/2lb red mullet or snapper
2 onions, sliced
1 green chilli, seeded and chopped
1 each red and green (bell)
  pepper, sliced
3 garlic cloves, crushed
15ml/1 tbsp tomato purée (paste)
50ml/2fl oz/¼ cup fish stock
5–6 tomatoes, peeled and sliced or
  400g/14oz can tomatoes
30ml/2 tbsp chopped fresh parsley
30ml/2 tbsp lemon juice
5ml/1 tsp paprika
15–20 green and black olives
salt and ground black pepper
bread and salad, to serve

1 Heat 30ml/2 tbsp of the oil in a large roasting pan or frying pan and cook the fish on both sides until golden brown. Remove the fish from the pan, cover and keep warm.

COOK'S TIP
One large fish looks spectacular, but can be tricky to cook and serve. If you prefer, buy four smaller fish and cook for a shorter time, until just tender and cooked through but not overdone.

2 Heat the remaining oil in the pan and cook the onions for 2–3 minutes, until slightly softened. Add the chilli and red and green peppers and continue cooking for 3–4 minutes, stirring occasionally, then add the garlic and stir-fry for a further minute.

3 Blend the tomato purée with the stock and stir into the pan with the tomatoes, parsley, lemon juice, paprika and seasoning. Simmer gently without boiling for 15 minutes, stirring occasionally.

4 Return the fish to the pan and cover with the sauce. Cook for 10 minutes, then add the olives and cook for a further 5 minutes, or until just cooked through.

5 Transfer the fish to a serving dish and pour the sauce over the top. Leave to cool, then cover and chill until completely cold. Serve cold with bread and salad.

KING PRAWNS IN CURRY SAUCE

SERVES 4

INGREDIENTS

  450g/1lb raw king prawns
    (jumbo shrimp)
  600ml/1 pint/2$^{1}/_{2}$ cups water
  3 thin slices fresh root ginger
  10ml/2 tsp curry powder
  2 garlic cloves, crushed
  15g/$^{1}/_{2}$ oz/1 tbsp butter or margarine
  60ml/4 tbsp ground almonds
  1 green chilli, seeded and finely
    chopped
  45ml/3 tbsp single (light) cream
  salt and ground black pepper

For the vegetables
  15ml/1 tbsp mustard oil
  15ml/1 tbsp vegetable oil
  1 onion, sliced
  $^{1}/_{2}$ red (bell) pepper, seeded and
    thinly sliced
  $^{1}/_{2}$ green (bell) pepper, seeded and
    thinly sliced
  1 christophene, peeled, stoned (pitted)
    and cut into strips
  salt and ground black pepper

1 Peel the prawns and place the shells in a pan with the water and ginger. Simmer, uncovered, for 15 minutes, until reduced by half. Strain into a jug (pitcher) and discard the shells.

2 Devein the prawns, place in a bowl and season with the curry powder, garlic and salt and pepper and set aside.

3 Heat the mustard and vegetable oils in a large frying pan, add all the vegetables and stir-fry for 5 minutes. Season with salt and pepper, spoon into a serving dish and keep warm.

4 Wipe out the frying pan, then melt the butter or margarine and sauté the prawns for about 5 minutes, until pink. Spoon over the bed of vegetables, cover and keep warm.

5 Add the ground almonds and chilli to the pan, stir-fry for a few seconds and then add the reserved stock and bring to the boil. Reduce the heat, stir in the cream and simmer for a few minutes, without boiling.

6 Pour the sauce over the vegetables and prawns before serving.

FRIED FISH IN GREEN CHILLI SAUCE

SERVES 4

INGREDIENTS

  4 medium pomfret
  juice of 1 lemon
  5ml/1 tsp garlic granules
  salt and ground black pepper
  vegetable oil, for shallow frying

For the coconut sauce
  450ml/$^{3}/_{4}$ pint/scant 2 cups water
  2 thin slices fresh root ginger
  25–40g/1–1$^{1}/_{2}$ oz creamed coconut
    or 120–175ml/4–6fl oz/$^{1}/_{2}$–$^{3}/_{4}$ cup
    coconut cream
  30ml/2 tbsp vegetable oil
  1 red onion, sliced
  2 garlic cloves, crushed
  1 green chilli, seeded and thinly sliced
  15ml/1 tbsp chopped fresh coriander
  salt and ground black pepper

1 Cut the fish in half and sprinkle inside and out with the lemon juice. Season with the garlic granules and salt and pepper and set aside to marinate for a few hours.

2 Heat a little oil in a large frying pan. Pat away the excess lemon juice from the fish, cook in the oil for 10 minutes, turning once. Set aside.

3 To make the sauce, place the water in a pan with the slices of ginger, bring to the boil and simmer until the liquid is reduced to just over 300ml/$^{1}/_{2}$ pint/1$^{1}/_{4}$ cups. Take out the ginger and reserve, then add the creamed coconut to the pan and stir until the coconut has melted.

4 Heat the oil in a wok or large pan and cook the onion and garlic for 2–3 minutes. Add the reserved ginger and coconut stock, the chilli and coriander, stir well and then gently add the fish. Simmer for 10 minutes, until the fish is cooked through. Transfer the fish to a warmed serving plate, adjust the seasoning for the sauce and pour over the fish. Serve immediately.

CHILLI CRABS

THERE ARE VARIATIONS ON THIS RECIPE ALL OVER ASIA, BUT ALL ARE HOT AND SPICY. THIS DELICIOUS DISH OWES ITS SPICINESS AND FLAVOUR TO CHILLIES, GINGER AND SHRIMP PASTE.

SERVES 4

INGREDIENTS

2 cooked crabs, about 675g/1¹/₂ lb
1cm/¹/₂ in cube shrimp paste
2 garlic cloves
2 fresh red chillies, seeded, or 5ml/
   1 tsp chopped chilli from a jar
1cm/¹/₂ in fresh root ginger, peeled
   and sliced
60ml/4 tbsp sunflower oil
300ml/¹/₂ pint/1¹/₄ cups tomato ketchup
15ml/1 tbsp dark brown sugar
150ml/¹/₄ pint/²/₃ cup warm water
4 spring onions (scallions), chopped,
   to garnish
cucumber chunks and hot toast,
   to serve (optional)

1 Remove the large claws of one crab and turn it on to its back, with the head facing away from you. Use your thumbs to push the body up from the main shell. Discard the stomach sac and the "dead men's fingers", i.e. lungs and any green matter. Leave the creamy brown meat in the shell and cut the shell in half, with a cleaver or strong knife. Cut the body section in half and crack the claws with a sharp blow from a hammer or cleaver. Avoid splintering the claws. Repeat with the other crab.

2 Grind the shrimp paste, garlic, fresh chillies and ginger to a paste using a mortar and pestle.

3 Heat a work and add the oil. Fry the spice paste, stirring it all the time, but without browning.

4 Stir in the tomato ketchup, sugar and water and mix the sauce well. When just boiling, add all the crab pieces and toss in the sauce until well-coated and hot. Serve in a large bowl, sprinkled with the spring onions. Place in the centre of the table for everyone to help themselves. Accompany this finger-licking dish with cool cucumber chunks and hot toast for mopping up the sauce, if you like.

CARIBBEAN SPICED FISH

THIS DISH IS OF SPANISH ORIGIN AND IS VERY POPULAR THROUGHOUT THE CARIBBEAN. THERE ARE AS MANY VARIATIONS OF THE NAME OF THE DISH AS THERE ARE WAYS OF PREPARING IT.

SERVES 4–6

INGREDIENTS
900g/2lb cod fillet
$^1/_2$ lemon
15ml/1 tbsp spice seasoning
flour, for dusting
oil, for frying
lemon wedges, to garnish

For the sauce
30ml/2 tbsp vegetable oil
1 onion, sliced
$^1/_2$ red (bell) pepper, sliced
$^1/_2$ chayote, peeled and stoned (pitted),
   cut into small pieces
2 garlic cloves, crushed
120ml/4fl oz/$^1/_2$ cup malt vinegar
75ml/5 tbsp water
2.5ml/$^1/_2$ tsp ground allspice
1 bay leaf
1 small Scotch Bonnet chilli, chopped
15ml/1 tbsp soft brown sugar
salt and ground black pepper

1 Place the fish in a shallow dish, squeeze over the lemon, then sprinkle with the spice seasoning and pat into the fish. Leave to marinate in a cool place for at least 1 hour.

COOK'S TIP
In the Caribbean, whole red snapper or red mullet are used for this dish.

2 Cut the fish fillet into 7.5cm/3in pieces and dust with a little flour, shaking off the excess.

3 Heat the oil in a heavy frying pan and cook the fish pieces for 2–3 minutes, until golden brown and crisp, turning occasionally. To make the sauce, heat the oil in a heavy frying pan and cook the onion until soft.

4 Add the pepper, chayote and garlic and stir-fry for 2 minutes. Pour in the vinegar, then add the remaining ingredients and simmer gently for 5 minutes. Leave to stand for 10 minutes, then pour the sauce over the fish. Serve hot, garnished with lemon wedges.

PRAWNS IN SPICY TOMATO SAUCE

CUMIN AND CINNAMON ADD SUBTLE SPICINESS TO THIS DELICIOUS, SIMPLE-TO-MAKE PRAWN RECIPE, WHICH COMES FROM THE MIDDLE EAST.

SERVES 4

INGREDIENTS
   30ml/2 tbsp oil
   2 onions, finely chopped
   2–3 garlic cloves, crushed
   5–6 tomatoes, peeled and chopped
   30ml/2 tbsp tomato purée (paste)
   120ml/4fl oz/^{1}/$_2$ cup fish stock
    or water
   2.5ml/^{1}/$_2$ tsp ground cumin
   2.5ml/^{1}/$_2$ tsp ground cinnamon
   450g/1 lb raw, peeled Mediterranean
    prawns (shrimp)
   juice of 1 lemon
   salt and ground black pepper
   fresh parsley, to garnish
   rice, to serve

1 Heat the oil in a large frying pan and cook the onions for 3–4 minutes, until golden. Add the garlic, cook for about 1 minute, and then stir in the tomatoes.

2 Blend the tomato purée with the stock or water and stir into the pan with the cumin, cinnamon and seasoning. Simmer, covered, over a low heat for 15 minutes, stirring occasionally. Do not allow to boil.

3 Add the prawns and lemon juice and simmer the sauce for 10–15 minutes more over a low to medium heat until the prawns are cooked and the stock is reduced by about half.

4 Serve with plain rice or in a decorative ring of Persian Rice, and garnished with fresh parsley.

SPICED FISH KEBABS

MARINATING ADDS SPICY FLAVOUR TO THESE DELICIOUS KEBABS.

SERVES 4–6

INGREDIENTS
   900g/2lb swordfish steaks
   45ml/3 tbsp olive oil
   juice of ^{1}/$_2$ lemon
   1 garlic clove, crushed
   5ml/1 tsp cayenne pepper
   3 tomatoes, quartered
   2 onions, cut into wedges
   salt and ground black pepper
   salad and pitta bread, to serve

COOK'S TIP
Almost any type of firm white fish can be used for this recipe.

1 Cut the fish into large cubes and place in a dish.

2 Blend together the oil, lemon juice, garlic, paprika and seasoning in a small mixing bowl and pour over the fish. Cover loosely with clear film (plastic wrap) and leave to marinate in a cool place for up to 2 hours.

3 Thread the fish cubes on to skewers, alternating them with pieces of tomato and onion.

4 Grill the kebabs over hot charcoal for 5–10 minutes, basting frequently with the remaining marinade and turning occasionally. Serve the kebabs with salad and pitta bread.

PRAWNS IN SPICED COCONUT SAUCE

SPICES, CHILLIES AND HERBS MAKE A FRAGRANT SAUCE FOR THIS DISH.

SERVES 4

INGREDIENTS
24–30 large raw prawns (shrimp)
spice seasoning, for dusting
juice of 1 lemon
30ml/2 tbsp butter or margarine
1 onion, chopped
2 garlic cloves, crushed
30ml/2 tbsp tomato purée (paste)
2.5ml/^{1}/$_2$ tsp dried thyme
2.5ml/^{1}/$_2$ tsp ground cinnamon
15ml/1 tbsp chopped coriander (cilantro)
^{1}/$_2$ hot chilli pepper, chopped
175g/6oz/1 cup frozen or canned corn
300ml/^{1}/$_2$ pint/1^1/$_4$ cups coconut milk
chopped fresh coriander, to garnish

1 Sprinkle the prawns with spice seasoning and lemon juice and marinate in a cool place for an hour.

2 Melt the butter or margarine in a pan. Cook the onion and garlic for 5 minutes, until slightly softened. Add the prawns and cook for a few minutes, stirring occasionally until cooked through and pink.

3 Transfer the prawns, onion and garlic to a bowl, leaving behind some of the buttery liquid. Add the tomato purée to the pan and cook over a low heat, stirring thoroughly. Add the thyme, cinnamon, coriander and hot pepper and stir well.

4 Blend the corn (reserving 15ml/1 tbsp) in a blender or food processor with the coconut milk. Add to the pan and simmer until reduced. Add the prawns and reserved corn, and simmer for 5 minutes. Serve hot, garnished with coriander.

COOK'S TIP
If you use raw king prawns (jumbo shrimp), make a stock from the shells and use in place of some of the coconut milk.

CURRIED PRAWNS AND SALTFISH

SHRIMP PASTE AND SPICES ADD TASTY FLAVOUR TO THIS FISH DISH.

SERVES 4

INGREDIENTS
450g/1 lb raw prawns (shrimp), peeled
15ml/1 tbsp spice seasoning
25g/1oz/2 tbsp butter or margarine
15ml/1 tbsp olive oil
2 shallots, finely chopped
1 garlic clove, crushed
350g/12oz okra, trimmed and cut into
   2.5cm/1 in lengths
5ml/1 tsp curry powder
10ml/2 tsp shrimp paste
15ml/1 tbsp chopped fresh
   coriander (cilantro)
15ml/1 tbsp lemon juice
175g/6oz prepared saltfish (see Cook's
   Tip), shredded

1 Season the prawns with the spice seasoning and leave to marinate in a cool place for about 1 hour.

2 Heat the butter or margarine and olive oil in a large frying pan or wok over a medium heat and stir-fry the shallots and garlic for 5 minutes. Add the okra, curry powder and shrimp paste, stir well and cook for about 10 minutes, until the okra is tender.

3 Add 30ml/2 tbsp water, coriander, lemon juice, prawns and saltfish, and cook gently for 5–10 minutes. Adjust the seasoning and serve hot.

COOK'S TIP
Soak the saltfish for 12 hours, changing the water two or three times. Rinse, bring to the boil in fresh water, then cool.

LEMON GRASS PRAWNS ON CRISP NOODLE CAKE

SERVES 4

INGREDIENTS

300g/11oz thin egg noodles
60ml/4 tbsp vegetable oil
500g/1¼lb raw king prawns (jumbo
  shrimp), peeled and deveined
2.5ml/½ tsp ground coriander
15ml/1 tbsp ground turmeric
2 garlic cloves, finely chopped
2 slices fresh root ginger,
  finely chopped
2 lemon grass stalks, finely chopped
2 shallots, finely chopped
15ml/1 tbsp tomato purée (paste)
250ml/8fl oz/1 cup coconut cream
4–6 kaffir lime leaves (optional)
15–30ml/1–2 tbsp fresh lime juice
15–30ml/1–2 tbsp fish sauce
1 cucumber, peeled, seeded and cut
  into 5cm/2in batons
1 tomato, seeded and cut into strips
2 red chillies, seeded and finely sliced
salt and ground black pepper
2 spring onions (scallions), finely
  sliced, and a few coriander (cilantro)
  sprigs, to garnish

1 Cook the egg noodles in a pan of boiling water until just tender. Drain, rinse under cold running water and drain well.

2 Heat 15ml/1 tbsp of the oil in a large frying pan. Add the noodles, distributing them evenly, and fry for 4–5 minutes until crisp and golden. Turn the noodle cake over and fry the other side. Alternatively, make four individual cakes. Keep hot.

3 In a bowl, toss the prawns with the ground coriander, turmeric, garlic, ginger and lemon grass. Add salt and pepper to taste.

4 Heat the remaining oil in a large frying pan. Add the shallots, cook for 1 minute, then add the prawns and cook for a further 2 minutes. Using a slotted spoon remove the prawns.

5 Stir the tomato purée and coconut cream into the mixture remaining in the pan. Stir in lime juice to taste and season with the fish sauce. Bring the sauce to a simmer, return the prawns to the sauce, then add the kaffir lime leaves, if using, and the cucumber. Simmer gently until the prawns are cooked and the sauce is reduced to a nice coating consistency.

6 Add the tomato, stir until just warmed through, then add the chillies. Serve on top of the crisp noodle cake(s), garnished with sliced spring onions and fresh coriander sprigs.

STIR-FRIED PRAWNS WITH TAMARIND

THE SOUR, TANGY FLAVOUR THAT IS CHARACTERISTIC OF MANY THAI DISHES COMES FROM TAMARIND. FRESH TAMARIND PODS FROM THE TAMARIND TREE CAN SOMETIMES BE BOUGHT, BUT PREPARING THEM FOR COOKING IS A LABORIOUS PROCESS. THE THAIS, HOWEVER, USUALLY PREFER TO USE COMPRESSED BLOCKS OF TAMARIND PASTE, WHICH IS SIMPLY SOAKED IN WARM WATER AND THEN STRAINED.

SERVES 4–6

INGREDIENTS

50g/2oz tamarind paste
150ml/¼ pint/⅔ cup boiling water
30ml/2 tbsp vegetable oil
30ml/2 tbsp chopped onion
30ml/2 tbsp palm sugar
30ml/2 tbsp chicken stock or water
15ml/1 tbsp fish sauce
6 dried red chillies, fried
450g/1lb raw shelled prawns (shrimp)
15ml/1 tbsp fried chopped garlic
30ml/2 tbsp fried sliced shallots
2 spring onions (scallions), chopped,
  to garnish

1 Put the tamarind paste in a small bowl, pour over the boiling water and stir well to break up any lumps. Leave for about 30 minutes. Strain the paste, pushing as much of the juice through as possible. Measure 90ml/6 tbsp of the juice, the amount needed, and store the remainder in the refrigerator. Heat the oil in a wok. Add the chopped onion and cook until golden brown.

2 Add the sugar, stock, fish sauce, dried chillies and the tamarind juice, stirring well until the sugar dissolves. Bring to the boil.

3 Add the prawns, garlic and shallots. Stir-fry until the prawns are cooked, about 3–4 minutes. Garnish with the spring onions.

SPICY PRAWNS WITH OKRA

SERVES 4–6

INGREDIENTS

60–90ml/4–6 tbsp oil
225g/8oz okra, washed, dried and
  left whole
4 garlic cloves, crushed
5cm/2in piece of fresh root
  ginger, chopped
4–6 green chillies, cut diagonally
2.5ml/$^1/_2$ tsp ground turmeric
4–6 curry leaves
5ml/1 tsp cumin seeds
450g/1lb raw king prawns (jumbo
  shrimp), peeled and deveined
10ml/2 tsp brown sugar
juice of 2 lemons
salt, to taste

1 Heat the oil in a frying pan and cook
the okra on a fairly high heat until they
are slightly crisp and browned on all
sides. Remove from the oil and keep
aside on a piece of kitchen paper.

2 In the same oil, gently cook the garlic,
ginger, chillies, turmeric, curry leaves and
cumin seeds for 2–3 minutes. Add the
prawns and mix well, then cook until
the prawns are tender.

3 Add the salt, sugar, lemon juice and
cooked okra. Increase the heat and
quickly cook for a further 5 minutes,
stirring gently to prevent the okra from
breaking. Adjust the seasoning, if
necessary. Serve hot.

COOK'S TIP
Okra should be cooked rapidly to
prevent the pods from breaking up
and releasing their distinctive thick,
sticky liquid.

SPICY PRAWNS WITH CORNMEAL

THESE CRISPY FRIED PRAWNS WITH A CORNMEAL COATING AND A CHEESE TOPPING ARE TRULY DELICIOUS WHEN SERVED WITH A SPICY TOMATO SALSA AND LIME WEDGES TO EASE THE HEAT.

SERVES 4

INGREDIENTS
115g/4oz/³/4 cup cornmeal
5–10ml/1–2 tsp cayenne pepper
2.5ml/¹/2 tsp ground cumin
5ml/1 tsp salt
30ml/2 tbsp chopped fresh coriander
 (cilantro) or parsley
900g/2lb large raw prawns (shrimp),
 peeled and deveined
flour, for dredging
¹/4 cup vegetable oil
115g/4oz/1 cup grated
 Cheddar cheese

To serve
 lime wedges
 tomato salsa

1 Preheat the grill (broiler). In a mixing bowl, combine the cornmeal, cayenne, cumin, salt and coriander or parsley.

2 Coat the prawns lightly in flour, then dip them in water and roll them in the cornmeal mixture to coat.

3 Heat the oil in a non-stick frying pan. When hot, add the prawns, in batches if necessary. Cook them until they are opaque throughout, for about 2–3 minutes on each side. Drain on kitchen paper.

4 Place the prawns in a large ovenproof dish, or in individual dishes. Sprinkle the cheese evenly over the top. Grill (broil) about 8cm/3in from the heat until the cheese melts, for about 2–3 minutes. Serve immediately, with lime wedges and tomato salsa.

PINEAPPLE CURRY WITH PRAWNS AND MUSSELS

THE DELICATE SWEET AND SOUR FLAVOUR OF THIS CURRY COMES FROM THE PINEAPPLE AND ALTHOUGH IT SEEMS AN ODD COMBINATION, IT IS RATHER DELICIOUS. USE THE FRESHEST SHELLFISH THAT YOU CAN FIND.

SERVES 4–6

INGREDIENTS
600ml/1 pint/2¹/₂ cups coconut milk
30ml/2 tbsp red curry paste
30ml/2 tbsp fish sauce
15ml/1 tbsp granulated sugar
225g/8oz king prawns (jumbo shrimp),
    peeled and deveined
450g/1lb mussels, scrubbed and
    beards removed
175g/6oz fresh pineapple, finely
    crushed or chopped
5 kaffir lime leaves, torn
2 red chillies, chopped, and coriander
    (cilantro) leaves, to garnish

1 In a large pan, bring half the coconut milk to the boil and heat it, stirring, until it separates.

2 Add the red curry paste and cook until fragrant. Add the fish sauce and sugar and continue to cook for a few moments.

4 Reheat until boiling and then simmer for 3–5 minutes, until the prawns are cooked and the mussels have opened. Remove any mussels that have not opened and discard. Serve garnished with chopped red chillies and coriander leaves.

3 Stir in the rest of the coconut milk and bring back to the boil. Add the king prawns, mussels, pineapple and kaffir lime leaves.

CURRIED PRAWNS IN COCONUT MILK

A CURRY-LIKE DISH WHERE THE PRAWNS ARE COOKED IN A SPICY COCONUT GRAVY.

SERVES 4–6

INGREDIENTS
600ml/1 pint/2¹/₂ cups coconut milk
30ml/2 tbsp yellow curry paste (see
    Cook's Tip)
15ml/1 tbsp fish sauce
2.5ml/¹/₂ tsp salt
5ml/1 tsp granulated sugar
450g/1lb king prawns (jumbo shrimp),
    peeled, tails left intact and deveined
225g/8oz cherry tomatoes
juice of ¹/₂ lime, to serve
2 red chillies, cut into strips, and
    coriander (cilantro) leaves, to garnish

1 Put half the coconut milk into a pan or wok and bring to the boil.

2 Add the yellow curry paste to the coconut milk, stir until it disperses, then simmer for about 10 minutes.

3 Add the fish sauce, salt, sugar and remaining coconut milk. Simmer for another 5 minutes.

4 Add the prawns and cherry tomatoes. Simmer very gently for about 5 minutes, until the prawns are pink and tender.

5 Serve sprinkled with lime juice and garnish with chillies and coriander.

COOK'S TIP
To make yellow curry paste, process together 6–8 yellow chillies, 1 chopped lemon grass stalk, 4 peeled shallots, 4 garlic cloves, 15ml/1 tbsp peeled chopped fresh root ginger, 5ml/1 tsp coriander seeds, 5ml/1 tsp mustard powder, 5ml/1 tsp salt, 2.5ml/¹/₂ tsp ground cinnamon, 15ml/1 tbsp light brown sugar and 30ml/2 tbsp oil in a blender or food procesor. When a paste has formed, transfer to a glass jar and keep in the refrigerator.

Meat and poultry dishes cooked with chillies and spices

are universally popular, but recipe variations are

endless, and each country adds its own twist and unique

mixture of spices; Blackened Hot Chicken from the Deep

South, Caribbean Barbecue Jerk Chicken, Beef

Enchiladas from Mexico and Spicy Meat Fritters from

Indonesia are just a few of the fiery dishes on offer.

Scorching Meat
and Poultry

SPICY MEAT FRITTERS

MAKES 30

INGREDIENTS
450g/1lb potatoes, boiled and drained
450g/1lb lean minced (ground) beef
1 onion, quartered
1 bunch spring onions
 (scallions), chopped
3 garlic cloves, crushed
5ml/1 tsp ground nutmeg
15ml/1 tbsp coriander seeds, dry-fried
 and ground
10ml/2 tsp cumin seeds, dry-fried
 and ground
4 eggs, beaten
oil, for shallow frying
salt and ground black pepper

1 While the potatoes are still warm, mash them in the pan until they are well broken up. Add to the minced beef and mix well.

2 Finely chop the onion, spring onions and garlic. Add to the meat with the ground nutmeg, coriander and cumin. Stir in enough beaten egg to give a soft consistency which can be formed into fritters. Season to taste.

3 Heat the oil in a large frying pan. Using a dessertspoon, scoop out 6–8 oval-shaped fritters and drop them into the hot oil. Leave to set, so that they keep their shape (this will take about 3 minutes) and then turn over and cook for a further minute.

4 Drain well on kitchen paper and keep warm while cooking the remaining fritters.

BARBECUE PORK SPARERIBS

SERVES 4

INGREDIENTS
1kg/2^1/4lb pork spareribs
1 onion
2 garlic cloves
2.5cm/1in fresh root ginger
75ml/3fl oz/^{1}/3 cup dark soy sauce
1–2 fresh red chillies, seeded
 and chopped
5ml/1 tsp tamarind pulp, soaked in
 75ml/5 tbsp water
15–30ml/1–2 tbsp dark brown sugar
30ml/2 tbsp groundnut (peanut) oil
salt and ground black pepper

1 Wipe the pork ribs and place them in a wok, wide frying pan or large flameproof casserole.

2 Finely chop the onion, crush the garlic and peel and slice the ginger. Blend the soy sauce, onion, garlic, ginger and chopped chillies together to a paste in a food processor or with a mortar and pestle. Strain the tamarind and reserve the juice. Add the tamarind juice, brown sugar, oil and seasoning to taste to the onion mixture and mix well together.

3 Pour the sauce over the ribs and toss well to coat. Bring to the boil and then simmer, uncovered and stirring frequently, for 30 minutes. Add extra water if necessary.

4 Put the ribs on a rack in a roasting pan, place under a preheated grill (broiler), on a barbecue or in the oven at 200°C/400°F/Gas 6 and continue cooking until the ribs are tender, about 20 minutes, depending on the thickness of the ribs. Baste the ribs with the sauce and turn them over occasionally.

BEEF WITH CACTUS PIECES

NOPALITOS — CHUNKS OF AN EDIBLE CACTUS — ARE USED AS A VEGETABLE IN MEXICO, AND ARE THE BASIS OF SEVERAL SALADS, SOUPS AND BAKED DISHES.

SERVES 6

INGREDIENTS

 900g/2lb braising beef, cut into
  5cm/2in cubes
 30ml/2 tbsp corn oil
 1 onion, finely chopped
 2 garlic cloves, chopped
 1 or 2 jalapeño chillies, seeded and
  chopped
 115g/4oz can nopalitos (cactus pieces),
  rinsed and drained
 2 x 275g/10oz cans tomatillos
  (Mexican green tomatoes)
 50g/2oz/^{1}/$_2$ cup chopped fresh
  coriander (cilantro)
 beef stock (optional)
 salt and ground black pepper
 chopped fresh coriander, to garnish

1 Pat the beef cubes dry with kitchen paper. Heat the oil in a frying pan and sauté the beef cubes, a few at a time, until browned all over. Using a slotted spoon, transfer the beef cubes to a flameproof casserole or pan.

2 Add the onion and garlic to the oil remaining in the frying pan and sauté until the onion is tender. Add more oil if necessary. Add the onions and garlic to the casserole or pan together with the chillies.

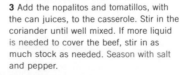

COOK'S TIP
Tomatillos (Mexican green tomatoes) are not to be confused with ordinary green unripe tomatoes. Look for them, canned, in speciality markets and food stores.

3 Add the nopalitos and tomatillos, with the can juices, to the casserole. Stir in the coriander until well mixed. If more liquid is needed to cover the beef, stir in as much stock as needed. Season with salt and pepper.

4 Bring to a slow simmer, cover and cook over a low heat for about 2^1/$_2$ hours, or until the beef is very tender. Serve sprinkled with the chopped coriander.

TEX-MEX BAKED POTATOES WITH CHILLI

SERVES 4

INGREDIENTS
  2 large potatoes
  15ml/1 tbsp oil
  1 garlic clove, crushed
  1 small onion, chopped
  1/2 red (bell) pepper, seeded and
    chopped
  225g/8oz/2 cups lean minced (ground) beef
  1/2 fresh red chilli, seeded and chopped
  5ml/1 tsp ground cumin
  pinch of cayenne pepper
  200g/7oz can chopped tomatoes
  30ml/2 tbsp tomato purée (paste)
  2.5ml/1/2 tsp dried oregano
  2.5ml/1/2 tsp dried marjoram
  200g/7oz can red kidney beans
  15ml/1 tbsp chopped coriander
    (cilantro)
  60ml/4 tbsp sour cream
  salt and ground black pepper
  chopped fresh parsley, to garnish

1 Preheat the oven to 220°C/425°F/
Gas 7. Oil the potatoes and pierce with
skewers. Bake for 30 minutes.

2 Heat the oil in a pan and add the garlic,
onion and pepper. Cook gently for about
4–5 minutes, until softened.

3 Add the minced beef and cook until
it is browned all over, then stir in the
chopped chilli, ground cumin, cayenne
pepper, tomatoes, tomato purée,
60ml/4 tbsp water and the herbs.
Cover the pan and simmer for about
25 minutes, stirring occasionally.

VARIATION
For a lower fat topping, use natural
(plain) yogurt instead of sour cream.

4 Drain the kidney beans and add to the
pan. Cook for 5 minutes, turn off the heat
and stir in the chopped coriander. Season
well and set aside.

5 Cut the baked potatoes in half and
place one half in each of four serving
bowls. Top each one with the chilli
beef mixture and a spoon of sour cream
and garnish with plenty of chopped
fresh parsley.

BEEF ENCHILADAS

SERVES 4

INGREDIENTS

900g/2lb braising steak
15ml/1 tbsp vegetable oil, plus extra
    for frying
5ml/1 tsp salt
5ml/1 tsp dried oregano
2.5ml/½ tsp ground cumin
1 onion, quartered
2 garlic cloves, crushed
1 litre/1³/4 pints/4 cups enchilada sauce
12 corn tortillas
115g/4oz/1 cup grated cheese
chopped spring onions (scallions), to garnish
sour cream, to serve

1 Preheat the oven to 160°C/325°F/
Gas 3. Place the meat on a sheet of foil
and rub it all over with the oil. Sprinkle
both sides with the salt, oregano and
cumin and rub in well. Add the onion and
garlic. Top with another sheet of foil and
roll up to seal the edges, leaving room for
some steam expansion during cooking.

2 Place in an ovenproof dish and bake for
3 hours, until the meat is tender enough
to shred. Remove from the foil and shred
the meat using two forks.

3 Stir 120ml/4fl oz/½ cup of the enchilada
sauce into the beef. Spoon a thin layer of
enchilada sauce on the base of a
rectangular ovenproof dish, or in four
individual dishes.

4 Place the remaining sauce in a frying
pan and warm gently.

5 Put a 1cm/½in layer of vegetable oil in
a second frying pan and heat until hot but
not smoking. With tongs, lower a tortilla
into the oil; the temperature is correct if it
just sizzles. Cook for 2 seconds, then turn
and cook the other side for 2 seconds. Lift
out, drain over the pan and then transfer
to the pan with the sauce. Dip in the
sauce just to coat both sides.

6 Transfer the softened tortilla
immediately to a plate. Spread about
2–3 spoonfuls of the beef mixture down
the centre of the tortilla. Roll it up and
place the filled tortilla, seam side down,
in the prepared dish. Repeat this process
for all the remaining tortillas.

7 Spoon the remaining sauce from the
frying pan over the beef enchiladas,
spreading it right down to the ends.
Sprinkle the grated cheese down the
centre.

8 Bake the enchiladas for about
10–15 minutes, until the cheese topping
just melts. Sprinkle with chopped spring
onions and serve immediately, with sour
cream on the side.

COOK'S TIP
For a quicker recipe, use minced
(ground) beef. Cook in a little oil with
chopped onion and garlic, until
browned all over. Continue the recipe
from step 3.

RED ENCHILADAS

SERVES 6

INGREDIENTS

    4 dried ancho chillies
    450g/1lb tomatoes, peeled, seeded
      and chopped
    1 onion, finely chopped
    1 garlic clove, chopped
    15ml/1 tbsp chopped fresh
      coriander (cilantro)
    lard or corn oil, for frying
    250ml/8fl oz/1 cup sour cream
    4 chorizo sausages, skinned and
      chopped
    18 freshly prepared unbaked
      corn tortillas
    50g/2oz/^{2}/3 cup freshly grated
      Parmesan cheese
    salt and ground black pepper

1 Roast the ancho chillies in a dry frying pan over a medium heat for 1–2 minutes, shaking the pan frequently. When cool, carefully slit the chillies, remove the stems and seeds, and tear the pods into pieces. Put in a bowl, add warm water to just cover, and soak for 20 minutes.

2 Tip the chillies, with a little of the soaking water, into a food processor. Add the tomatoes, onion, garlic and coriander and process.

COOK'S TIP
The method of dipping the tortillas first in sauce, then quickly cooking them in lard or oil gives the best flavour. If you prefer, fry the plain tortillas very quickly, then dip them in the sauce, stuff and roll. There is not a great loss of flavour, and no spatter.

3 Heat 15ml/1 tbsp lard or oil in a pan. Add the purée and cook gently over a medium heat, stirring, for 3–4 minutes. Season to taste with salt and pepper and then stir in the sour cream. Remove the pan from the heat and set it aside.

4 Heat a further 15ml/1 tbsp lard or oil in a small frying pan, and sauté the chorizo for a few minutes until lightly browned. Moisten with a little of the sauce and set the pan aside.

5 Preheat the oven to 180°C/350°F/ Gas 4. Heat 30ml/2 tbsp lard or oil in a frying pan. Dip a tortilla in the sauce and add to the pan. Cook for a few seconds, shaking the pan gently, turn over and briefly fry the other side.

6 Slide the tortilla on to a plate, top with some of the sausage mixture, and roll up. Pack the prepared tortillas in a single layer in an ovenproof dish. Pour the sauce over, sprinkle with Parmesan and bake for about 20 minutes.

CARIBBEAN LAMB CURRY

THIS POPULAR NATIONAL DISH OF JAMAICA IS KNOWN AS CURRY GOAT ALTHOUGH GOAT MEAT OR LAMB CAN BE USED TO MAKE IT.

SERVES 4–6

INGREDIENTS

900g/2lb boned leg of lamb
60ml/4 tbsp curry powder
3 garlic cloves, crushed
1 large onion, chopped
4 thyme sprigs or 1 teaspoon dried thyme
3 bay leaves
5ml/1 tsp ground allspice
30ml/2 tbsp vegetable oil
50g/2oz/¼ cup butter or margarine
900ml/1½ pints/3¾ cups stock
  or water
1 fresh hot chilli, chopped
cooked rice, to serve
coriander (cilantro) sprigs, to garnish

1 Cut the meat into 5cm/2in cubes, discarding any excess fat and gristle.

2 Place the lamb, curry powder, garlic, onion, thyme, bay leaves, allspice and oil in a large bowl and mix well. Leave to marinate in the refrigerator for at least 3 hours or overnight.

COOK'S TIP
Try goat, or mutton, if you can and enjoy a robust curry.

3 Melt the butter or margarine in a large heavy pan, add the seasoned lamb and cook over a medium heat for about 10 minutes, turning the meat frequently.

4 Stir in the stock and chilli and bring to the boil. Reduce the heat, cover the pan and simmer for 1½ hours, or until the meat is tender. Serve with rice, garnish with coriander.

LAMB STEW

This stew is known as Estofado de Carnero *in Mexico. The recipe for this dish has an interesting mix of chillies — the mild, full-flavoured ancho, and the piquant jalapeño which gives extra "bite". The heat of the chillies is mellowed by the addition of ground cinnamon and cloves. Boneless neck fillet is very good for this dish, as it is lean, tender, flavoursome and inexpensive.*

SERVES 4

INGREDIENTS

3 dried ancho chillies
30ml/2 tbsp olive oil
1 jalapeño chilli, seeded and
   chopped
1 onion, finely chopped
2 garlic cloves, chopped
450g/1lb tomatoes, peeled
   and chopped
50g/2oz/¹/₃ cup seedless raisins
1.5ml/¹/₄ tsp ground cinnamon
1.5ml/¹/₄ tsp ground cloves
900g/2lb boneless lamb, cut into
   5cm/2in cubes
250ml/8fl oz/1 cup lamb stock
   or water
salt and ground black pepper
a few sprigs of fresh coriander
   (cilantro), to garnish
coriander rice, to serve

COOK'S TIP
To make coriander (cilantro) rice,
simply heat 30ml/2 tbsp corn oil in
a large frying pan and gently cook
1 finely chopped onion for about
8 minutes, or until soft but not brown.
Stir in enough cooked, long grain rice
for four and stir gently over a medium
heat until heated through. Sprinkle
over 30–45ml/2–3 tbsp chopped fresh
coriander and stir in thoroughly.

1 Roast the ancho chillies lightly in a dry frying pan over a low heat to bring out their flavour.

2 Remove the stems, shake out the seeds and tear the pods into pieces, then put them into a bowl. Pour in enough warm water to just cover. Leave to soak for 30 minutes.

3 Heat the olive oil in a frying pan and sauté the jalapeño chilli together with the onion and garlic until the onion is tender.

4 Add the chopped tomatoes to the pan and cook until the mixture is thick and well blended. Stir in the raisins, ground cinnamon and cloves, and season to taste with salt and black pepper. Transfer the mixture to a flameproof casserole.

5 Tip the ancho chillies and their soaking water into a food processor and process to a smooth purée. Add the chilli purée to the tomato mixture in the casserole.

6 Add the lamb cubes to the casserole, stir to mix and pour in enough of the lamb stock or water to just cover the meat.

7 Bring to a simmer, then cover the casserole and cook over a low heat for about 2 hours, or until the lamb is tender. Garnish with fresh coriander and serve with coriander rice.

SWEET AND SOUR PORK

SERVES 4

INGREDIENTS

350g/12oz lean pork
1.5ml/¼ tsp salt and 2.5ml/½ tsp
 ground Sichuan peppercorns
15ml/1 tbsp Chinese rice wine
115g/4oz bamboo shoots
30ml/2 tbsp plain (all-purpose) flour
1 egg, lightly beaten
vegetable oil, for frying
15ml/1 tbsp vegetable oil
1 garlic clove, finely chopped
1 spring onion (scallion), cut into
 short sections
1 small green (bell) pepper, diced
 finely
1 fresh red chilli, seeded and shredded
15ml/1 tbsp light soy sauce
30ml/2 tbsp light brown sugar
45ml/3 tbsp rice vinegar
15ml/1 tbsp tomato purée (paste)
about 120ml/4fl oz/½ cup stock

1 Using a sharp knife, cut the lean pork into small bitesize cubes. Marinate with the salt, ground peppercorns and Chinese wine for about 15–20 minutes.

2 Cut the bamboo shoots into small cubes about the same size as the pork pieces.

3 Dust the pork with flour, dip in the beaten egg, and coat with more flour. Deep-fry in moderately hot oil for 3–4 minutes, stirring to separate the pieces. Remove.

4 Reheat the oil, add the pork and bamboo shoots and fry for 1 minute, or until golden. Drain.

5 Heat 15ml/1 tbsp oil and add the garlic, spring onion, pepper and chilli. Stir-fry for 30–40 seconds, then add the seasonings with the stock. Bring to the boil, then add the pork and bamboo shoots and heat through. Serve.

LAMB TAGINE WITH CORIANDER AND SPICES

THIS IS A VERSION OF A MOROCCAN-STYLE TAGINE IN WHICH CHOPS ARE SPRINKLED WITH SPICES AND EITHER MARINATED FOR A FEW HOURS OR COOKED STRAIGHTAWAY.

SERVES 4

INGREDIENTS

4 lamb chump (leg) chops
2 garlic cloves, crushed
pinch of saffron threads
2.5ml/½ tsp ground cinnamon,
    plus extra to garnish
2.5ml/½ tsp ground ginger
15ml/1 tbsp chopped fresh
    coriander (cilantro)
15ml/1 tbsp chopped fresh parsley
1 onion, finely chopped
45ml/3 tbsp olive oil
300ml/½ pint/1¼ cups lamb stock
50g/2oz/½ cup blanched almonds, to
    garnish
5ml/1 tsp sugar
salt and ground black pepper

1 Season the lamb with the garlic, saffron, cinnamon, ginger and a little salt and black pepper. Place on a large plate and sprinkle with the coriander, parsley and onion. Cover loosely and set aside in the refrigerator for a few hours to marinate.

COOK'S TIP
Lamb tagine is a fragrant dish, originating in North Africa. It is traditionally made in a cooking dish, known as a tagine, from where it takes its name. This dish consists of a plate with a tall lid with sloping sides. It has a narrow opening to let steam escape, while retaining the flavour.

2 Heat the oil in a large frying pan, over a medium heat. Add the marinated lamb and all the herbs and onion from the dish.

3 Cook for 1–2 minutes, turning once, then add the stock, bring to the boil and simmer gently for 30 minutes, turning the chops once.

4 Meanwhile, heat a small frying pan over a medium heat, add the almonds and dry-fry until golden, shaking the pan occasionally to make sure they colour evenly. Transfer to a bowl and set aside.

5 Transfer the chops to a serving plate and keep warm. Increase the heat under the pan and boil the sauce until reduced by about half. Stir in the sugar. Pour the sauce over the chops and sprinkle with the fried almonds and a little extra ground cinnamon.

KHARA MASALA LAMB

WHOLE SPICES ARE USED IN THIS CURRY SO YOU SHOULD WARN THE DINERS OF THEIR PRESENCE IN ADVANCE! IT IS DELICIOUS WHEN SERVED WITH FRESHLY BAKED NAAN BREAD OR A RICE ACCOMPANIMENT. THIS DISH IS BEST MADE WITH GOOD-QUALITY SPRING LAMB.

SERVES 4

INGREDIENTS
    75ml/5 tbsp corn oil
    2 onions, chopped
    5ml/1 tsp shredded ginger
    6 whole dried red chillies
    3 cardamom pods
    2 cinnamon sticks
    6 black peppercorns
    3 cloves
    2.5ml/$\frac{1}{2}$ tsp salt
    450g/1lb boned leg of lamb, cubed
    600ml/1 pint/2$\frac{1}{2}$ cups water
    2 fresh green chillies, sliced
    30ml/2 tbsp chopped fresh
       coriander (cilantro)

1 Heat the oil in a large pan. Lower the heat slightly and cook the onions until they are lightly browned.

2 Add half the ginger and half the garlic and stir well.

3 Throw in half the red chillies, the cardamoms, cinnamon, peppercorns, cloves and salt.

4 Add the lamb and cook over a medium heat. Stir constantly with a semi-circular movement, using a wooden spoon to scrape the base of the pan. Continue in this way for about 5 minutes.

5 Pour in the water, cover with a lid and cook over a medium-low heat for 35–40 minutes, or until the water has evaporated and the meat is tender.

6 Add the rest of the shredded ginger, sliced garlic and the whole dried red chillies, along with the sliced fresh green chillies and the chopped fresh coriander.

COOK'S TIP
The action of stirring the meat and spices together using a semi-circular motion, as described in step 4, is called bhoono-ing. It makes sure that the meat becomes well-coated and combined with the spice mixture before the cooking liquid is added.

7 Continue to stir over the heat until you see some free oil on the sides of the pan. Transfer to a serving dish and serve immediately.

DEEP-FRIED SPARERIBS WITH SPICY SALT AND PEPPER

IF YOU WANT THESE SPARERIBS TO BE HOTTER, JUST INCREASE THE AMOUNT OF CHILLI SAUCE.

SERVES 4–6

INGREDIENTS
10–12 finger ribs, in total about
   675g/1½ lb, with excess fat and
   gristle trimmed
about 30–45ml/2–3 tbsp flour
vegetable oil, for deep-frying
For the marinade
1 garlic clove, crushed and chopped
15ml/1 tbsp light brown sugar
15ml/1 tbsp dark soy sauce
30ml/2 tbsp Chinese rice wine or
   dry sherry
2.5ml/½ tsp chilli sauce
few drops sesame oil

1 Chop each rib into 3–4 pieces. Combine all the marinade ingredients in a bowl, add the spareribs and leave to marinate for at least 2–3 hours.

2 Coat the spareribs with flour and deep-fry them in medium-hot oil for about 4–5 minutes, stirring to separate. Remove from the pan and drain.

3 Heat the oil to high and deep-fry the spareribs once more for about 1 minute, or until the colour is an even dark brown. Remove and drain, then serve hot.

SPICY SALT AND PEPPER
To make Spicy Salt and Pepper, mix 15ml/1 tbsp salt with 10ml/2 tsp ground Sichuan peppercorns and 5ml/1 tsp fivespice powder. Heat together in a preheated dry pan for about 2 minutes over a low heat, stirring constantly. This quantity is sufficient for at least six servings.

PORK WITH CHILLIES AND PINEAPPLE

SERVES 6

INGREDIENTS

30ml/2 tbsp corn oil
900g/2lb boneless pork shoulder or
  loin, cut into 5cm/2in cubes
1 onion, finely chopped
1 large red (bell) pepper, seeded and
  finely chopped
1 or more jalapeño chillies, seeded and
  finely chopped
450g/1lb fresh pineapple chunks
8 fresh mint leaves, chopped
250ml/8fl oz/1 cup chicken stock
salt and ground black pepper
fresh mint sprig, to garnish
rice, to serve

1 Heat the oil in a large frying pan and sauté the pork, in batches, until the cubes are lightly coloured. Transfer the pork to a flameproof casserole, leaving the oil behind in the pan.

2 Add the finely chopped onion, finely chopped red pepper and the chilli(es) to the oil remaining in the pan. Sauté until the onion is tender, then add to the casserole with the pineapple. Stir to mix.

3 Add the mint, then cover and simmer gently for about 2 hours, or until the pork is tender. Garnish with fresh mint and serve with rice.

COOK'S TIP
If fresh pineapple is not available, use pineapple canned in its own juice.

MOLE POBLANO DE GUAJOLOTE

MOLE POBLANO DE GUAJOLOTE IS THE GREAT FESTIVE DISH OF MEXICO. IT IS SERVED AT ANY SPECIAL OCCASION, BE IT A BIRTHDAY, WEDDING, OR FAMILY GET-TOGETHER. RICE, BEANS, TORTILLAS AND GUACAMOLE ARE THE TRADITIONAL ACCOMPANIMENTS.

SERVES 6–8

INGREDIENTS

2.75–3.6kg/6–8lb turkey, cut into
   serving pieces
1 onion, chopped
1 garlic clove, chopped
90ml/6 tbsp lard or corn oil
salt
fresh coriander (cilantro) and
   30ml/2 tbsp toasted sesame seeds,
   to garnish

For the sauce
  6 dried ancho chillies
  4 dried pasilla chillies
  4 dried mulato chillies
  1 drained canned chipotle chilli,
    seeded and chopped (optional)
  2 onions, chopped
  2 garlic cloves, chopped
  450g/1lb tomatoes, peeled
    and chopped
  1 stale tortilla, torn into pieces
  50g/2oz/$^1/_3$ cup seedless raisins
  115g/4oz/1 cup ground almonds
  45ml/3 tbsp sesame seeds, ground
  2.5ml/$^1/_2$ tsp coriander seeds, ground
  5ml/1 tsp ground cinnamon
  2.5ml/$^1/_2$ tsp ground anise
  1.5ml/$^1/_4$ tsp ground black peppercorns
  60ml/4 tbsp lard or corn oil
  40g/1$^1/_2$oz unsweetened (bitter)
    chocolate, broken into squares
  15ml/1 tbsp sugar
salt and ground pepper

1 Put the turkey pieces into a pan or flameproof casserole large enough to hold them in one layer comfortably. Add the onion and garlic, and enough cold water to cover. Season with salt, bring to a gentle simmer, cover and cook for about 1 hour, or until the turkey is tender.

2 Meanwhile, put the ancho, pasilla and mulato chillies in a dry frying pan over a low heat and roast them for a few minutes, shaking the pan frequently. Remove the stems and shake out the seeds. Tear the pods into pieces and put these into a small bowl. Add sufficient warm water to just cover and soak, turning occasionally, for 30 minutes, until they are soft.

3 Lift out the turkey pieces and pat them dry with kitchen paper. Reserve the stock in a measuring jug (cup). Heat the lard or oil in a large frying pan and sauté the turkey pieces until lightly browned all over. Transfer to a plate and set aside. Reserve the oil that is left in the pan.

4 Tip the chillies, with the water in which they have been soaked, into a food processor. Add the chipotle chilli, if using, with the onions, garlic, tomatoes, tortilla, raisins, ground almonds and spices. Process to a purée. Do this in batches if necessary.

5 Add the lard or oil to the fat remaining in the frying pan used for sautéing the turkey. Heat the mixture, then add the chilli and spice paste. Cook, stirring, for 5 minutes.

6 Transfer the mixture to the pan or casserole in which the turkey was originally cooked. Stir in 475ml/16fl oz/ 2 cups of the turkey stock (make it up with water if necessary). Add the chocolate and season with salt and pepper. Cook over a low heat until the chocolate has melted. Stir in the sugar. Add the turkey and more stock if needed. Cover the pan and simmer very gently for 30 minutes. Serve, garnished with fresh coriander and sprinkled with the sesame seeds.

COOK'S TIP

Lightly roasting the dried chillies brings out their flavour and is well worth the extra effort. Take care not to burn them.

SPICY MEATBALLS

SERVE THESE INDONESIAN MEATBALLS WITH A SAMBAL OR A SPICY SAUCE.

MAKES 24

INGREDIENTS

1 large onion, coarsely chopped
1–2 fresh red chillies, seeded
  and chopped
2 garlic cloves, crushed
1cm/½in cube shrimp paste
15ml/1 tbsp coriander seeds
5ml/1 tsp cumin seeds
450g/1lb lean minced (ground) beef
10ml/2 tsp dark soy sauce
5ml/1 tsp dark brown sugar
juice of ½ lemon
a little beaten egg
oil, for shallow frying
salt and ground black pepper
fresh coriander (cilantro) sprigs,
  to garnish

1 Put the onions, chillies, garlic and shrimp paste in a food processor. Process but do not over-chop or the onion will become too wet and spoil the consistency of the meatballs. Dry-fry the coriander and cumin seeds in a preheated pan for about 1 minute, to release the aroma. Do not brown. Grind them with a mortar and pestle.

2 Put the meat in a large bowl. Stir in the onion mixture. Add the ground coriander and cumin, soy sauce, seasoning, sugar and lemon juice. Bind with a little beaten egg and shape into small, even-size balls.

3 Chill the meatballs briefly to firm up, if necessary. Fry in shallow oil, turning often, until cooked through and browned. This will take 4–5 minutes, depending on their size.

4 Remove from the pan, drain well on kitchen paper and serve, garnished with coriander sprigs.

BEEF AND AUBERGINE CURRY

SERVES 6

INGREDIENTS

120ml/4fl oz/½ cup sunflower oil
2 onions, thinly sliced
2.5cm/1in fresh root ginger, sliced and
  cut into batons
1 garlic clove, crushed
2 fresh red chillies, seeded and very
  finely sliced
2.5cm/1 in fresh turmeric, peeled and
  crushed, or 5ml/1 tsp ground turmeric
1 lemon grass stalk, lower part sliced
  finely, top bruised
675g/1½lb braising steak, cut in even-
  size strips
400ml/14fl oz can coconut milk
300ml/½ pint/1¼ cups water
1 aubergine (eggplant), sliced and
  patted dry
5ml/1 tsp tamarind pulp, soaked in
  60ml/4 tbsp warm water
salt and ground black pepper
finely sliced chilli and deep-fried
  onions, to garnish
boiled rice, to serve

1 Heat half the oil and cook the onions, ginger and garlic until they give off a rich aroma. Add the chillies, turmeric and the lower part of the lemon grass. Push to one side and then turn up the heat and add the steak, stirring until the meat changes colour.

COOK'S TIP
If you want to make this curry, Gulai Terung Dengan Daging, ahead, prepare to the end of step 2 and finish later.

2 Add the coconut milk, water, lemon grass top and seasoning to taste. Cover and simmer gently for 1½ hours, or until the meat is tender.

3 Towards the end of the cooking time heat the remaining oil in a frying pan. Cook the aubergine slices until brown on both sides.

4 Add the browned aubergine slices to the beef curry and cook for a further 15 minutes. Stir gently occasionally. Strain the tamarind and stir the juice into the curry. Taste and adjust the seasoning. Put into a warm serving dish. Garnish with the sliced chilli and deep-fried onions and serve with boiled rice.

SPICY FRIED CHICKEN

THIS CRISPY CHICKEN IS SUPERB HOT OR COLD. SERVED WITH A SALAD OR VEGETABLES, IT MAKES A DELICIOUS LUNCH AND IS IDEAL FOR PICNICS OR SNACKS TOO.

SERVES 4–6

INGREDIENTS

    4 chicken drumsticks
    4 chicken thighs
    10ml/2 tsp curry powder
    2.5ml/$\frac{1}{2}$ tsp garlic granules
    2.5ml/$\frac{1}{2}$ tsp ground black pepper
    2.5ml/$\frac{1}{2}$ tsp paprika
    about 300ml/$\frac{1}{2}$ pint/1$\frac{1}{4}$ cups milk
    oil, for deep frying
    50g/2oz/4 tbsp plain (all-purpose) flour
    salt
    salad leaves, to serve

1 Place the chicken pieces in a large bowl and sprinkle with the curry powder, garlic granules, black pepper, paprika and salt. Rub the spices well into the chicken, then cover and leave to marinate in a cool place for at least 2 hours, or overnight in the refrigerator.

2 Preheat the oven to 180°C/350°F/ Gas 4. Pour enough milk into the bowl to cover the chicken and leave to stand for a further 15 minutes.

3 Heat the oil in a large pan or deep-fat fryer and tip the flour on to a plate. Shake off excess milk, dip each piece of chicken in flour and fry two or three pieces at a time until golden, but not cooked. Continue until all the chicken is fried.

4 Remove with a slotted spoon, place the chicken pieces on a baking sheet, and bake for about 30 minutes. Serve hot or cold with salad.

SPICY CHICKEN WITH COCONUT

TRADITIONALLY, THE CHICKEN PIECES FOR THIS INDONESIAN DISH WOULD BE PART-COOKED BY FRYING, BUT ROASTING THEM IN THE OVEN IS JUST AS SUCCESSFUL. THIS RECIPE IS UNUSUAL IN THAT IT DOES NOT CONTAIN ANY CHILLIES OR TURMERIC, BUT GALANGAL, LEMON GRASS, CORIANDER AND LIME LEAVES ADD A SPICY FLAVOUR.

SERVES 4–6

INGREDIENTS

1.5kg/3–3½lb chicken or
  4 chicken quarters
4 garlic cloves
1 onion, sliced
4 macadamia nuts or 8 almonds
15ml/1 tbsp coriander seeds, dry-fried,
  or 5ml/1 tsp ground coriander
45ml/3 tbsp oil
2.5cm/1in fresh galangal, peeled
  and bruised
2 lemon grass stalks, fleshy part bruised
3 lime leaves
2 bay leaves
5ml/1 tsp sugar
600ml/1 pint/2½ cups coconut milk
salt
boiled rice and deep-fried onions,
  to serve

1 Preheat the oven to 190°C/375°F/ Gas 5. Cut the chicken into four or eight pieces. Season with salt. Place it in an oiled roasting pan and cook in the oven for 25–30 minutes. Meanwhile, prepare the sauce.

2 Grind the garlic, onion, nuts and coriander to a fine paste in a food processor or with a mortar and pestle. Heat the oil and fry the paste to bring out the flavour. Do not allow it to brown.

3 Add the part-cooked chicken to a wok, with the galangal, lemon grass, lime and bay leaves, sugar, coconut milk and salt to taste. Mix well to coat in the sauce.

4 Bring to the boil then reduce the heat and simmer gently for 30–40 minutes, uncovered, until the chicken is tender and the coconut sauce is reduced and thickened. Stir the mixture occasionally during cooking.

5 Just before serving, remove the bruised galangal and lemon grass. Serve with boiled rice sprinkled with crisp deep-fried onions.

CRISPY AND AROMATIC DUCK

AS THIS DISH IS OFTEN SERVED WITH PANCAKES, SPRING ONIONS, CUCUMBER AND DUCK SAUCE (A SWEET BEAN PASTE), MANY PEOPLE MISTAKE IT FOR PEKING DUCK. THIS RECIPE, HOWEVER, USES A DIFFERENT COOKING METHOD. THE RESULT IS JUST AS CRISPY BUT THE DELIGHTFUL AROMA MAKES THIS DISH PARTICULARLY DISTINCTIVE. PLUM SAUCE MAY BE SUBSTITUTED FOR THE DUCK SAUCE.

SERVES 6–8

INGREDIENTS

 1 oven-ready duckling,
 about 2.25kg/5–5¼lb
 10ml/2 tsp salt
 5–6 whole star anise
 15ml/1 tbsp Sichuan peppercorns
 5ml/1 tsp cloves
 2–3 cinnamon sticks
 3–4 spring onions (scallions)
 3–4 slices fresh root ginger, unpeeled
 75–90ml/5–6 tbsp Chinese rice wine
 or dry sherry
 vegetable oil, for deep-frying
 lettuce leaves, to garnish

To serve
 Chinese pancakes
 duck sauce
 spring onions, shredded
 cucumber, diced

1 Remove the wings from the duck and split the body in half down the backbone.

2 Rub salt all over the two duck halves, taking care to work it all in thoroughly.

3 Marinate the duck in a dish with the spices, spring onions, fresh ginger and wine or sherry for at least 4–6 hours.

4 Vigorously steam the duck with the marinade for 3–4 hours (or for longer if possible). Carefully remove the steamed duck from the cooking liquid and leave to cool for at least 5–6 hours. The duck must be cold and dry or the skin will not be crisp.

5 Heat the vegetable oil in a wok until it is just smoking, then place the duck pieces in the oil, skin side down. Deep-fry the duck for about 5–6 minutes, or until it becomes crisp and brown. Turn the duck just once at the very last moment.

6 Remove the fried duck, drain it well and place it on a bed of lettuce leaves.

7 To serve, scrape the meat off the bone and wrap a portion in each pancake with a little duck sauce, shredded spring onions and cucumber. It is traditional to eat it with your fingers.

COOK'S TIP
Small pancakes suitable for this recipe can be found in most Chinese supermarkets. They can be frozen and will keep for up to 3 months in the freezer.

BARBECUE JERK CHICKEN

JERK REFERS TO THE BLEND OF HERB AND SPICE SEASONING RUBBED INTO MEAT, BEFORE IT IS ROASTED OVER CHARCOAL SPRINKLED WITH PIMIENTO BERRIES. IN JAMAICA, JERK SEASONING WAS ORIGINALLY USED ONLY FOR PORK, BUT JERKED CHICKEN IS EQUALLY GOOD AND NOW VERY POPULAR.

SERVES 4

INGREDIENTS
    8 chicken pieces
For the marinade
    5ml/1 tsp ground allspice
    5ml/1 tsp ground cinnamon
    5ml/1 tsp dried thyme
    1.5ml/¼ tsp freshly grated nutmeg
    10ml/2 tsp demerara (raw) sugar
    2 garlic cloves, crushed
    15ml/1 tbsp finely chopped onion
    15ml/1 tbsp chopped spring
       onion (scallion)
    15ml/1 tbsp vinegar
    30ml/2 tbsp oil
    15ml/1 tbsp lime juice
    1 hot chilli, chopped
    salt and ground black pepper
    salad leaves, to serve

1 Combine all the marinade ingredients in a small bowl. Using a fork, mash them together well to form a thick paste.

2 Lay the chicken pieces on a plate or board and make several lengthways slits in the flesh. Rub the seasoning all over the chicken and into the slits.

3 Place the chicken pieces in a dish, cover with clear film (plastic wrap) and marinate overnight in the refrigerator.

4 Shake off any excess seasoning from the chicken. Brush with oil and either place on a baking sheet or on a barbecue grill. Cook under a preheated grill (broiler) for 45 minutes, turning frequently. Alternatively, for the barbecue, light the coals and when ready, cook over the coals for 30 minutes, turning frequently. Serve hot with salad leaves.

COOK'S TIP
The flavour is best if you marinate the chicken overnight. Sprinkle the charcoal with aromatic herbs, such as bay leaves, for even more flavour.

BLACKENED HOT CHICKEN

SERVES 6

INGREDIENTS

6 skinless boneless chicken
  breast portions
75g/3oz/6 tbsp butter or margarine
5ml/1 tsp garlic powder
10ml/2 tsp onion powder
5ml/1 tsp cayenne pepper
10ml/2 tsp sweet paprika
7.5ml/1 1/2 tsp salt
2.5ml/1/2 tsp ground white pepper
5ml/1 tsp ground black pepper
1.5ml/1/4 tsp ground cumin
5ml/1 tsp dried thyme

1 Slice each chicken breast piece in half horizontally, making two pieces of about the same thickness. Flatten slightly with the heel of your hand.

2 Melt the butter or margarine in a small pan.

4 Heat a large heavy frying pan over a high heat until a drop of water sprinkled on the surface sizzles. This will take about 5–8 minutes.

3 Combine all the remaining ingredients in a shallow bowl and stir to blend together well. Brush the chicken pieces on both sides with melted butter or margarine, then sprinkle evenly with the seasoning mixture.

5 Drizzle 5ml/1 tsp melted butter on each chicken piece. Place them in the pan in an even layer, two or three at a time. Cook for 2–3 minutes, until the underside begins to blacken. Turn and cook the other side for another 2–3 minutes. Serve hot.

HOT CHICKEN CURRY

THIS CURRY HAS A NICE THICK SAUCE, AND USING RED AND GREEN PEPPERS GIVES IT EXTRA COLOUR.
IT CAN BE SERVED WITH EITHER WHOLEMEAL CHAPATIS OR PLAIN BOILED RICE.

SERVES 4

INGREDIENTS
30ml/2 tbsp corn oil
1.5ml/¼ tsp fenugreek seeds
1.5ml/¼ tsp onion seeds
2 onions, chopped
2.5ml/½ tsp garlic pulp
2.5ml/½ tsp ginger pulp
5ml/1 tsp ground coriander
5ml/1 tsp chilli powder
5ml/1 tsp salt
400g/14oz/1¾ cups canned tomatoes
30ml/2 tbsp lemon juice
350g/12oz/2½ cups skinned, boned
   and cubed chicken
30ml/2 tbsp chopped coriander
   (cilantro)
3 fresh green chillies, chopped
½ red (bell) pepper, cut into chunks
½ green (bell) pepper, cut into chunks
fresh coriander sprigs

2 Meanwhile, in a separate bowl, mix together the ground coriander, chilli powder, salt, canned tomatoes and lemon juice.

3 Pour this mixture into the pan and turn up the heat to medium. Stir-fry for about 3 minutes.

5 Add the fresh coriander, green chillies and the red and green peppers. Lower the heat, cover the pan and simmer for about 10 minutes, until the chicken is cooked.

6 Serve hot, garnished with fresh coriander sprigs.

COOK'S TIP
For a milder version of this delicious chicken curry, simply omit some of the fresh green chillies.

1 In a medium pan, heat the oil and fry the fenugreek and onion seeds until they turn a shade darker. Add the chopped onions, garlic and ginger and cook for about 5 minutes, until the onions turn golden brown. Turn the heat to very low.

4 Add the chicken pieces and stir-fry for 5–7 minutes.

SPATCHCOCKED DEVILLED POUSSINS

ENGLISH MUSTARD ADDS A HOT TOUCH TO THE SPICE PASTE USED IN THIS TASTY RECIPE.

SERVES 4

INGREDIENTS

15ml/1 tbsp English (hot) mustard powder
15ml/1 tbsp paprika
15ml/1 tbsp ground cumin
20ml/4 tsp tomato ketchup
15ml/1 tbsp lemon juice
65g/2½oz/5 tbsp butter, melted
4 poussins, about 450g/1lb each
salt

1 In a mixing bowl, combine the English mustard, paprika, ground cumin, tomato ketchup, lemon juice and salt. Mix together until smooth, then gradually stir in the melted butter until incorporated.

2 Using game shears or a strong pair of kitchen scissors, split each poussin along one side of the backbone, then cut down the other side of the backbone to remove it.

3 Open out a poussin, skin side uppermost, then press down firmly with the heel of your hand. Pass a long skewer through one leg and out through the other to secure the bird open and flat. Repeat with the remaining birds.

4 Spread the spicy mustard mixture evenly over the skin of each of the poussins. Cover them loosely and leave in a cool place for at least 2 hours. Preheat the grill (broiler).

5 Place the prepared poussins, skin side uppermost, on a grill rack and grill (broil) them for about 12 minutes. Turn the birds over and baste with any juices in the pan. Cook the poussins for a further 7 minutes, until all the juices run clear.

COOK'S TIP
Spatchcocked (butterflied) poussins cook very well on the barbecue. Make sure that the coals are very hot, then cook the birds for 15–20 minutes, turning and basting them frequently as they cook.

BON-BON CHICKEN WITH SPICY SESAME

IN THIS RECIPE, THE CHICKEN MEAT IS TENDERIZED BY BEING BEATEN WITH A STICK (CALLED A "BON" IN CHINESE) — HENCE THE NAME FOR THIS VERY POPULAR SICHUAN DISH.

INGREDIENTS

1 whole chicken, about 1kg/2¼lb
1.2 litres/2 pints/5 cups water
15ml/1 tbsp sesame oil
shredded cucumber, to garnish

For the sauce
30ml/2 tbsp light soy sauce
5ml/1 tsp sugar
15ml/1 tbsp finely chopped
  spring onions (scallions)
5ml/1 tsp red chilli oil
2.5ml/½ tsp Sichuan peppercorns
5ml/1 tsp white sesame seeds
30ml/2 tbsp sesame paste, or
  30ml/2 tbsp peanut butter creamed
  with a little sesame oil

1 Clean the chicken well. In a wok or pan bring the water to a rolling boil, add the chicken, reduce the heat, cover and cook for 40–45 minutes. Remove the chicken and immerse in cold water to cool.

2 After at least 1 hour, remove the chicken and drain. Dry it well with kitchen paper and brush with sesame oil. Carve the meat from the legs, wings and breast and pull the meat off the rest of the bones.

3 On a flat surface, pound the meat with a rolling pin, then tear the meat into shreds with your fingers.

4 Place the meat in a dish with the shredded cucumber around the edge. In a bowl, mix together all the sauce ingredients, keeping a few of the spring onions to garnish. Pour over the chicken and serve.

COOK'S TIP
To make chilli oil, slit and blanch chillies, pack into sterilized jars and fill with oil. Leave for 2 weeks.

CHICKEN SAUCE PIQUANTE

RED CHILLI PEPPERS ADD HEAT TO THIS CAJUN RECIPE. SAUCE PIQUANTE IS COMMONLY USED IN LOTS OF RECIPES TO LIVEN UP MEAT AND FISH AND GIVE MEALS A SPICY TASTE.

SERVES 4

INGREDIENTS

    4 chicken legs or 2 legs and
      2 breast portions
    75ml/5 tbsp oil
    50g/2oz/$\frac{1}{2}$ cup plain (all-purpose) flour
    1 onion, chopped
    2 celery sticks, sliced
    1 green (bell) pepper, seeded and diced
    2 garlic cloves, crushed
    1 bay leaf
    2.5ml/$\frac{1}{2}$ tsp dried thyme
    2.5ml/$\frac{1}{2}$ tsp dried oregano
    1–2 red chillies, seeded and finely chopped
    400g/14oz can tomatoes, chopped,
      with their juice
    300ml/$\frac{1}{2}$ pint/1$\frac{1}{4}$ cups chicken stock
    salt and ground black pepper
    watercress, to garnish
    boiled potatoes, to serve

COOK'S TIP
If you prefer to err on the side of caution when it comes to chilli heat, use just 1 chilli and hot up the seasoning at the end with a dash or two of Tabasco sauce.

2 In a heavy frying pan, cook the chicken pieces in the oil until brown on all sides, lifting them out and setting them aside as they are done.

3 Strain the oil from the pan into a heavy flameproof casserole. Heat it and stir in the flour. Stir constantly over a low heat until the roux is the colour of peanut butter.

4 As soon as the roux reaches the right stage, tip in the onion, celery and pepper and stir over the heat for 2–3 minutes.

5 Add the garlic, bay leaf, thyme, oregano and chilli or chillies. Stir for 1 minute, then turn down the heat and stir in the tomatoes with their juice.

6 Return the casserole to the heat and gradually stir in the stock. Add the chicken pieces, cover and simmer for 45 minutes, until the chicken is tender.

7 If there is too much sauce or it is too runny, remove the lid for the last 10–15 minutes of the cooking time and raise the heat a little.

8 Check the seasoning and serve garnished with watercress and accompanied by boiled potatoes, or perhaps rice or pasta, and a green vegetable or salad of your choice.

1 Halve the chicken legs through the joint, or the breast portions across the middle, to give eight pieces.

VARIATION
Any kind of meat, poultry or fish can be served with Sauce Piquante. Just cook the meat or fish first, then serve it with plenty of the sauce.

TANDOORI CHICKEN

SERVES 4

INGREDIENTS
    4 chicken quarters
    175ml/6fl oz/$^3/_4$ cup natural (plain)
        low-fat yogurt
    5ml/1 tsp garam masala
    5ml/1 tsp ginger pulp
    5ml/1 tsp garlic pulp
    7.5ml/1$^1/_2$ tsp chilli powder
    1.5ml/$^1/_4$ tsp ground turmeric
    5ml/1 tsp ground coriander
    15ml/1 tbsp lemon juice
    5ml/1 tsp salt
    few drops red food colouring
    30ml/2 tbsp corn oil
    mixed salad leaves, lime wedges and
        1 tomato, quartered, to garnish

1 Skin, rinse and pat dry the chicken quarters. Make two slits into the flesh of each piece, place them in a dish and set aside.

2 Mix together the yogurt, garam masala, ginger, garlic, chilli powder, turmeric, ground coriander, lemon juice, salt, red colouring and oil, and beat so that all the ingredients are well mixed together.

3 Cover the chicken quarters with the spice mixture and leave to marinate for about 3 hours.

4 Preheat the oven to 240°C/475°F/ Gas 9. Transfer the chicken pieces to an ovenproof dish.

5 Bake in the preheated oven for 20–25 minutes, or until the chicken is cooked right through and browned on top.

6 Remove from the oven, transfer to a serving dish and garnish with the salad leaves, lime and tomato.

COOK'S TIP
The red food colouring gives this dish its traditional appearance, but it can be omitted if you prefer.

SPICY MASALA CHICKEN

THESE CHICKEN PIECES ARE GRILLED AND HAVE A SWEET-AND-SOUR TASTE. THEY CAN BE SERVED COLD WITH A SALAD AND RICE, OR HOT WITH MASALA MASHED POTATOES.

SERVES 6

INGREDIENTS

    12 chicken thighs
    90ml/6 tbsp lemon juice
    5ml/1 tsp ginger pulp
    5ml/1 tsp garlic pulp
    5ml/1 tsp crushed dried red chillies
    5ml/1 tsp salt
    5ml/1 tsp soft brown sugar
    30ml/2 tbsp clear honey
    30ml/2 tbsp chopped fresh coriander
      (cilantro)
    1 fresh green chilli, finely chopped
    30ml/2 tbsp vegetable oil
    fresh coriander sprigs, to garnish

1 Prick all the chicken thighs with a fork. Rinse, pat dry and set aside in a bowl.

2 In a large mixing bowl, mix together the lemon juice, ginger, garlic, crushed dried red chillies, salt, sugar and honey.

3 Transfer the chicken thighs to the spice mixture and coat well. Set aside for about 45 minutes.

4 Preheat the grill (broiler) to medium. Add the fresh coriander and chopped green chilli to the chicken thighs and place them in a flameproof dish.

5 Pour any remaining marinade over the chicken and baste with the oil, using a pastry brush.

6 Grill (broil) the chicken thighs under the preheated grill for 15–20 minutes, turning and basting occasionally, until cooked through and browned.

7 Transfer to a serving dish and garnish with the fresh coriander sprigs.

COOK'S TIP
Masala refers to the blend of spices used in this dish. The amounts can be varied according to taste.

Vegetables have a mild flavour which makes them

perfect partners for assertive spices and hot chillies.

Potatoes will never seem bland again after Potatoes

with Red Chillies – this dish is for serious chilli

addicts. Have fun with Mexican recipes such as

Black Bean Burritos and Frijoles, which is simply

cooked beans spiked with serrano chillies.

Hot and Vibrant Vegetables and Salads

SICHUAN SPICY TOFU

SICHUAN PEPPER ADDS A SPICY, WOODY AROMA TO TOFU IN THIS DISH.

SERVES 4

INGREDIENTS

1 packet tofu
1 leek
115g/4oz/1 cup minced (ground) beef
45ml/3 tbsp vegetable oil
15ml/1 tbsp black bean sauce
15ml/1 tbsp light soy sauce
5ml/1 tsp chilli bean sauce
15ml/1 tbsp Chinese rice wine
  or dry sherry
about 45–60ml/3–4 tbsp water or
  vegetable stock
10ml/2 tsp cornflour (cornstarch) paste
ground Sichuan peppercorns, to taste
few drops sesame oil

1 Cut the tofu into 1cm/½in cubes and blanch them in a pan of boiling water for about 2–3 minutes, until they harden. Remove and drain. Cut the leek into short sections.

2 Stir-fry the minced beef in oil until the colour changes, then add the chopped leek and black bean sauce. Add the tofu with the soy sauce, chilli bean sauce and wine or sherry. Stir gently for 1 minute.

3 Add the vegetable stock or water, bring to the boil and braise for about 2–3 minutes.

4 Thicken the spicy sauce with the cornflour paste, season with the ground Sichuan peppercorns and sprinkle with some drops of sesame oil. Serve immediately.

POTATOES WITH RED CHILLIES

THE QUANTITY OF RED CHILLIES USED IN THIS POTATO DISH MAY BE TOO FIERY FOR SOME PALATES. IF YOU WOULD PREFER TO MAKE A MILDER VERSION, YOU COULD EITHER SEED THE RED CHILLIES, USE FEWER OF THEM OR JUST REPLACE THEM WITH A ROUGHLY CHOPPED RED PEPPER INSTEAD.

SERVES 4

INGREDIENTS
12–14 small new potatoes, halved
30ml/2 tbsp vegetable oil
2.5ml/½ tsp crushed dried red chillies
2.5ml/½ tsp white cumin seeds
2.5ml/½ tsp fennel seeds
2.5ml/½ tsp crushed coriander seeds
15ml/1 tbsp salt
1 onion, sliced
1–4 fresh red chillies, halved
  lengthways
15ml/1 tbsp chopped fresh
  coriander (cilantro)

COOK'S TIP
Serve this dish with plenty of cooling yogurt or raita, and some naan or chapatis.

1 Boil the halved new potatoes in a pan of salted water until they are soft but still firm to the touch. Remove them from the heat and drain off the water.

2 In a deep frying pan, heat the oil, then turn down the heat to medium. Add the crushed chillies, cumin, fennel and coriander seeds and salt and fry for 30–40 seconds.

3 Add the sliced onion and cook until it is golden brown. Then add the potatoes, fresh chillies and chopped fresh coriander.

4 Cover and cook for 5–7 minutes over a very low heat. Serve hot.

GREEN CHILLI DHAL

THIS DHAL (TARKA DHAL) IS PROBABLY THE MOST POPULAR OF LENTIL DISHES AND IS FOUND IN MOST INDIAN AND PAKISTANI RESTAURANTS.

SERVES 4

INGREDIENTS
   115g/4oz/½ cup masoor dhal (split red lentils)
   50g/2oz/¼ cup moong dhal (small split yellow lentils)
   600ml/1 pint/2½ cups water
   5ml/1 tsp ginger pulp
   5ml/1 tsp garlic pulp
   1.5ml/¼ tsp ground turmeric
   2 fresh green chillies, chopped
   7.5ml/1½ tsp salt

For the tarka
   30ml/2 tbsp oil
   1 onion, sliced
   1.5ml/¼ tsp mixed mustard and onion seeds
   4 dried red chillies
   1 tomato, sliced

To garnish
   15ml/1 tbsp chopped fresh coriander (cilantro)
   1–2 fresh green chillies, seeded and sliced
   15ml/1 tbsp chopped fresh mint

1 Pick over the lentils for any stones before washing them.

2 Boil the lentils in the water with the ginger, garlic, turmeric and chopped green chillies for about 15–20 minutes, until soft.

3 Mash the lentil mixture down. The consistency of the mashed lentils should be similar to that of a creamy chicken soup.

4 If the mixture looks too dry, just add some more water. Season with the salt.

5 To prepare the tarka, heat the oil and cook the onion with the mustard and onion seeds, dried red chillies and sliced tomato for 2 minutes.

6 Pour the tarka over the dhal and garnish with fresh coriander, green chillies and mint.

COOK'S TIP
Dried red chillies are available in many different sizes. If the ones you have are large, or if you want a less spicy flavour, reduce the quantity specified to 1–2.

FRIJOLES

<u>SERVES 6–8</u>

INGREDIENTS

350g/12oz/1³/4 cups dried red kidney,
   pinto or black haricot beans, picked
   over and rinsed
2 onions, finely chopped
2 garlic cloves, chopped
1 bay leaf
1 or more serrano chillies (small fresh
   green chillies)
30ml/2 tbsp corn oil
2 tomatoes, peeled, seeded
   and chopped
salt
sprigs of fresh bay leaves, to garnish

COOK'S TIP

In Yucatan black haricot beans are
cooked with the Mexican herb *epazote*.

1 Put the beans into a pan and add
cold water to cover by 2.5cm/1in.

2 Add half the onion, half the garlic, the
bay leaf and the chilli(es). Bring to the
boil and boil vigorously for about
10 minutes. Put the beans and liquid into
an earthenware pot or large pan, cover
and cook over a low heat for 30 minutes.
Add boiling water if the mixture starts to
become dry.

3 When the beans begin to wrinkle, add
15ml/1 tbsp of the corn oil and cook for a
further 30 minutes, or until the beans are
tender. Add salt to taste and cook for
30 minutes more, but do not add any
more water.

4 Remove the beans from the heat. Heat
the remaining oil in a small frying pan and
sauté the remaining onion and garlic until
the onion is soft. Add the tomatoes and
cook for a few minutes more.

5 Spoon 45ml/3 tbsp of the beans out
of the pot or pan and add them to the
tomato mixture. Mash to a paste. Stir
this into the beans to thicken the liquid.
Cook for just long enough to heat through,
if necessary. Serve the beans in small
bowls and garnish with sprigs of fresh
bay leaves.

BLACK BEAN BURRITOS

SERVES 4

INGREDIENTS

175g/6oz/1 cup dried black beans,
  soaked overnight and drained
1 bay leaf
45ml/3 tbsp sea salt
1 small red onion, chopped
225g/8oz/2 cups grated cheese
45ml/3 tbsp chopped pickled jalapeños
15ml/1 tbsp chopped coriander (cilantro)
750ml/1¼ pints/3 cups tomato salsa
8 flour tortillas
diced avocado, to serve

1 Place the beans in a large pan. Add
cold water to cover and the bay leaf.
Bring to the boil, then cover, and simmer
for 30 minutes. Add the salt and continue
simmering for about 30 minutes, until
tender. Drain and cool slightly. Discard
the bay leaf.

2 Preheat the oven to 180°C/350°F/ Gas
4. Grease a rectangular ovenproof
dish well.

3 In a mixing bowl, combine the beans,
onion, half the cheese, the jalapeños,
coriander and one-third of the salsa. Stir
to blend, then season.

4 Place one tortilla on a clean work
surface. Spread a large spoonful of the
filling down the middle, then roll it up to
enclose the filling completely. Place the
burrito in the prepared dish, seam side
down. Repeat this process with the
remaining tortillas until the dish is full.

5 Sprinkle the remaining cheese over the
burritos, in an even line right down the
middle. Bake in the oven for about 15
minutes, or until the cheese melts
completely.

6 Serve the bean burritos immediately,
with diced avocado and the
remaining salsa.

CHILLI COURGETTES

Calabacitas is an extremely easy recipe to make. If the cooking time seems unduly long, this is because the acid present in the tomatoes slows down the cooking of the courgettes. Use young tender courgettes.

SERVES 4

INGREDIENTS

   30ml/2 tbsp corn oil
   450g/1lb young courgettes (zucchini), sliced
   1 onion, finely chopped
   2 garlic cloves, chopped
   450g/1lb tomatoes, peeled, seeded
     and chopped
   2 drained canned jalapeño chillies,
     rinsed, seeded and chopped
   15ml/1 tbsp chopped fresh
     coriander (cilantro)
   salt
   fresh coriander, to garnish

1 Heat the oil in a flameproof casserole and add all the remaining ingredients, except the salt.

2 Bring to simmering point, cover and cook over a low heat for about 30 minutes, until the courgettes are tender, checking from time to time that the dish is not drying out. If it is, add a little tomato juice, stock or water.

3 Season with salt and serve the Mexican way as a separate course. Alternatively, serve with any plainly cooked meat or poultry. Garnish with fresh coriander.

REFRIED BEANS (FRIJOLES REFRITOS)

There is much disagreement about the translation of the term refrito. It means, literally, twice fried. Some cooks say this implies that the beans must be really well fried, others that it means twice cooked. However named, Frijoles Refritos are delicious.

SERVES 6–8

INGREDIENTS

   90–120ml/6–8 tbsp lard or corn oil
   1 onion, finely chopped
   1 quantity Frijoles (cooked beans)

To garnish
   freshly grated Parmesan cheese or
     crumbled cottage cheese
   crisp fried corn tortillas, cut
     into quarters

1 Heat 30ml/2 tbsp of the lard or oil in a large, heavy frying pan and sauté the onion until it is soft. Add about 225ml/ 8fl oz/1 cup of the frijoles (cooked beans).

COOK'S TIP
Lard is the traditional (and best tasting) fat for the beans but many people prefer to use corn oil. Avoid using olive oil, which is too strongly flavoured and distinctive.

2 Mash the beans with the back of a wooden spoon or potato masher, adding more beans and melted lard or oil until all the ingredients are used up and the beans have formed a heavy paste. Use extra lard or oil if necessary.

3 Tip out on to a warmed platter, piling the mixture up in a roll. Garnish with the cheese. Spike with the tortilla triangles, placing them at intervals along the length of the roll. Serve as a side dish.

SPICY CARROTS

ADDING SPICES TO THE CARROTS BEFORE LEAVING THEM TO COOL INFUSES THEM WITH FLAVOUR — AN IDEAL DISH TO SERVE COLD THE NEXT DAY (OR UP TO A WEEK LATER, IF YOU KEEP THEM IN THE REFRIGERATOR).

SERVES 4

INGREDIENTS
    450g/1lb carrots
    475ml/16fl oz/2 cups water
    2.5ml/$\frac{1}{2}$ tsp salt
    5ml/1 tsp cumin seeds
    $\frac{1}{2}$–1 red chilli (to taste)
    1 large garlic clove, crushed
    30ml/2 tbsp olive oil
    5ml/1 tsp paprika
    juice of 1 lemon
    flat leaf parsley, to garnish

1 Cut the carrots into slices about 5mm/$\frac{1}{4}$in thick. Bring the water to the boil and add the salt and carrot slices. Simmer for about 8 minutes, or until the carrots are just tender, without allowing them to get too soft. Drain the carrots, put them into a bowl and set aside.

2 Grind or crush the cumin to a powder. Remove the seeds from the chilli and chop the chilli finely. Take care when handling as they can irritate the skin and eyes.

3 Gently heat the oil in a pan and toss in the garlic and the chilli. Stir over a medium heat for about a minute, without allowing the garlic to brown. Stir in the paprika and the lemon juice.

4 Pour the warm mixture over the carrots, tossing them well so they are coated with the spices. Spoon into a serving dish and garnish with a sprig of flat leaf parsley.

KENYAN MUNG BEAN STEW

*THE KENYAN NAME FOR THIS
SIMPLE AND TASTY STEW IS* DENGU.

SERVES 4

INGREDIENTS

225g/8oz/1¼cups mung beans,
  soaked overnight
25g/1oz/2 tbsp ghee or butter
2 garlic cloves, crushed
1 red onion, chopped
30ml/2 tbsp tomato purée (paste)
½ green (bell) pepper, seeded and cut
  into small cubes
½ red (bell) pepper, seeded and cut
  into small cubes
1 green chilli, seeded and
  finely chopped
300ml/½ pint/1¼ cups water

1 Put the mung beans in a large pan,
cover with water and boil until the beans
are soft and the water has evaporated.
Remove from the heat and mash coarsely
with a fork or potato masher.

2 Heat the ghee or butter in a separate
pan, add the garlic and onion and cook
for 4–5 minutes, until golden brown, then
add the tomato purée and cook for a
further 2–3 minutes, stirring constantly.

3 Stir in the mashed beans, then the
green and red peppers and chilli.

4 Add the water, stirring well to mix all the
ingredients together.

5 Pour back into a clean pan and simmer
for about 10 minutes, then spoon into a
serving dish and serve immediately.

COOK'S TIP
If you prefer a more traditional,
smoother texture, cook the mung
beans until they are very soft, then
mash them thoroughly until smooth.

BROAD BEANS IN HOT SAUCE

A TASTY DISH OF LIMA BEANS WITH A TOMATO AND CHILLI SAUCE.

SERVES 4

INGREDIENTS

450g/1lb green lima or broad (fava)
  beans, thawed if frozen
30ml/2 tbsp olive oil
1 onion, finely chopped
2 garlic cloves, chopped
350g/12oz tomatoes, peeled, seeded
  and chopped
1 or 2 drained canned jalapeño
  chillies, seeded and chopped
salt
chopped fresh coriander (cilantro)
  sprigs, to garnish

1 Cook the beans in a pan of boiling water for 15–20 minutes, until tender. Drain and keep hot, to one side, in the covered pan.

2 Heat the olive oil in a frying pan and sauté the onion and garlic until the onion is soft but not brown. Add the tomatoes and cook until the mixture is thick and flavoursome.

3 Add the jalapeños and cook for 1–2 minutes. Season with salt.

4 Pour the mixture over the reserved beans and check that they are hot. If not, return everything to the frying pan and cook over a low heat for just long enough to heat through. Put into a warm serving dish, garnish with the coriander and serve.

BROAD BEAN AND CAULIFLOWER CURRY

THIS IS A HOT AND SPICY VEGETABLE CURRY, IDEAL WHEN SERVED WITH COOKED RICE (ESPECIALLY A BROWN BASMATI VARIETY), SMALL POPPADUMS AND MAYBE A COOLING CUCUMBER RAITA AS WELL.

SERVES 4

INGREDIENTS
2 garlic cloves, chopped
2.5cm/1 in cube fresh root ginger
1 fresh green chilli, seeded and
  chopped
15ml/1 tbsp oil
1 onion, sliced
1 large potato, chopped
30ml/2 tbsp ghee or softened butter
15ml/1 tbsp curry powder, mild or hot
1 cauliflower, cut into small florets
600ml/1 pint/2½ cups stock
30ml/2 tbsp creamed coconut or
  coconut cream
275g/10oz can broad (fava) beans
juice of ½ lemon (optional)
salt and ground black pepper
fresh coriander (cilantro), chopped,
  to garnish

1 Blend the garlic, ginger, chilli and oil in a food processor or blender until they form a smooth paste.

2 In a large pan, cook the onion and potato in the ghee or butter for 5 minutes, then stir in the spice paste and curry powder. Cook for 1 minute.

3 Add the cauliflower florets and stir well into the spicy mixture, then pour in the stock. Bring to the boil and then mix in the coconut, stirring until it melts and is well combined.

4 Season well, then cover and simmer for 10 minutes. Add the beans and their can juices and cook, uncovered, for a further 10 minutes.

5 Check the seasoning and add a good squeeze of lemon juice, if you like. Serve hot, garnished with the chopped coriander.

MASALA MASHED POTATOES

THESE POTATOES ARE VERY VERSATILE AND WILL PERK UP ANY MEAL.

SERVES 4

INGREDIENTS
- 3 potatoes
- 15ml/1 tbsp chopped fresh mint and coriander (cilantro), mixed
- 5ml/1 tsp mango powder
- 5ml/1 tsp salt
- 5ml/1 tsp crushed black peppercorns
- 1 fresh red chilli, chopped
- 1 fresh green chilli, chopped
- 50g/2oz/4 tbsp margarine

VARIATION
Instead of potatoes, try sweet potatoes. Cook them until tender, mash and continue from step 2.

1 Boil the potatoes until they are soft enough to be mashed. Mash them using a fork or potato masher.

2 Blend together the chopped herbs, mango powder, salt, pepper, chillies and margarine to form a paste.

3 Stir the mixture into the mashed potatoes and mix together thoroughly with a fork. Serve the potatoes warm, as an accompaniment.

SPICY CABBAGE

AN EXCELLENT VEGETABLE ACCOMPANIMENT, THIS IS A VERY VERSATILE SPICY DISH THAT CAN ALSO BE SERVED AS A WARM SIDE SALAD. IT'S SO QUICK TO MAKE THAT IT CAN BE A HANDY LAST MINUTE ADDITION TO ANY MEAL.

SERVES 4

INGREDIENTS
- 50g/2oz/4 tbsp margarine
- 2.5ml/½ tsp white cumin seeds
- 3–8 dried red chillies, to taste
- 1 small onion, sliced
- 225g/8oz/2½ cups shredded cabbage
- 2 carrots, grated
- 2.5ml/½ tsp salt
- 30ml/2 tbsp lemon juice

1 Melt the margarine in a pan and stir-fry the white cumin seeds and dried red chillies for about 30 seconds.

2 Add the sliced onion and cook for about 2 minutes. Add the cabbage and carrots and stir-fry for a further 5 minutes, until the cabbage is soft.

3 Finally, stir in the salt and lemon juice and serve.

VINEGARED CHILLI CABBAGE

A HOT CABBAGE DISH THAT WILL CERTAINLY ADD A BIT OF SPICE TO EVERY MEAL. THE ADDITION OF VINEGAR AT THE END GIVES THIS DISH ITS DISTINCT FLAVOUR.

SERVES 4–6

INGREDIENTS

1 fresh red chilli, halved, seeded
   and shredded
25g/1oz/2 tbsp lard or butter
2 garlic cloves, crushed (optional)
1 white cabbage, cored and shredded
10ml/2 tsp cider vinegar
5ml/1 tsp cayenne pepper
salt

1 Put the chilli with the lard or butter into a large pan and cook over a medium heat until the chilli sizzles and curls at the edges.

2 Add the garlic and cabbage and stir, over the heat, until the cabbage is coated and warm. Add salt to taste and 75ml/ 5 tbsp water. Bring to the boil, cover and lower the heat.

3 Cook, shaking the pan regularly, for about 3–4 minutes, until the cabbage wilts. Remove the lid, raise the heat and cook off the liquid. Check the seasoning and sprinkle with cider vinegar and cayenne pepper.

COOK'S TIP
A wok with a domed lid is good for this part-frying, part-steaming method of cooking cabbage.

COLESLAW IN TRIPLE-HOT DRESSING

THE TRIPLE HOTNESS IN THIS COLESLAW IS SUPPLIED BY MUSTARD, HORSERADISH AND TABASCO.

SERVES 6

INGREDIENTS

½ white cabbage, cored and shredded
2 celery sticks, finely sliced
1 green (bell) pepper, seeded and
   finely sliced
4 spring onions (scallions), shredded
30ml/2 tbsp chopped fresh dill
cayenne pepper

For the dressing
15ml/1 tbsp Dijon mustard
10ml/2 tsp creamed horseradish
5ml/1 tsp Tabasco sauce
30ml/2 tbsp red wine vinegar
75ml/5 tbsp olive oil
salt and ground black pepper

1 Mix the cabbage, celery, pepper and spring onions in a salad bowl.

2 Mix the mustard, horseradish and Tabasco sauce, then gradually stir in the vinegar with a fork and finally beat in the oil and seasoning. Toss the salad in the dressing and leave to stand, if possible, for at least 1 hour, turning once or twice.

3 Immediately before serving, season the salad if necessary, toss again and sprinkle with dill and cayenne.

COOK'S TIP
This is a good salad for a buffet table or picnic as it improves after standing in its dressing (it could be left overnight in the refrigerator) and travels well in a covered plastic bowl or box.

VEGETABLES IN PEANUT AND CHILLI SAUCE

<u>SERVES 4</u>

INGREDIENTS

15ml/1 tbsp palm or vegetable oil
1 onion, chopped
2 garlic cloves, crushed
400g/14oz can tomatoes, puréed
45ml/3 tbsp smooth peanut butter,
  preferably unsalted
750ml/1¼ pint/3²/₃ cups water
5ml/1 tsp dried thyme
1 green chilli, seeded and chopped
1 vegetable stock (bouillon) cube
2.5ml/½ tsp ground allspice
2 carrots
115g/4oz white cabbage
175g/6oz okra
½ red (bell) pepper
150ml/¼ pint/²/₃ cup vegetable stock
salt

1 Heat the oil in a large pan and cook the onion and garlic over a medium heat for 5 minutes, stirring frequently. Add the tomatoes and peanut butter and stir well.

2 Stir in the water, thyme, chilli, stock cube, allspice and a little salt. Bring to the boil, lower the heat and then simmer gently, uncovered for about 35 minutes.

3 Cut the carrots into sticks, slice the cabbage, trim the okra and seed and slice the red pepper.

4 Place the vegetables in a pan with the stock, bring to the boil and cook until tender but still with a little "bite".

5 Drain the vegetables and place in a warmed serving dish. Pour the sauce over the top and serve.

MARINATED VEGETABLES ON SKEWERS

THESE KEBABS ARE A DELIGHTFUL MAIN DISH FOR VEGETARIANS, OR SERVE THEM AS A VEGETABLE SIDE DISH.

SERVES 4

INGREDIENTS

115g/4oz pumpkin
1 red onion
1 small courgette (zucchini)
1 ripe plantain
1 aubergine (eggplant)
$^1/_2$ red (bell) pepper, seeded
$^1/_2$ green (bell) pepper, seeded
12 button (white) mushrooms
60ml/4 tbsp lemon juice
60ml/4 tbsp olive or sunflower oil
45–60ml/3–4 tbsp soy sauce
150ml/$^1/_4$ pint/$^2/_3$ cup tomato juice
1 green chilli, seeded and chopped
$^1/_2$ onion, grated
3 garlic cloves, crushed
7.5ml/1$^1/_2$ tsp dried tarragon, crushed
4ml/$^3/_4$ tsp dried basil
4ml/$^3/_4$ tsp dried thyme
4ml/$^3/_4$ tsp ground cinnamon
25g/1oz/2 tbsp butter or margarine
300ml/$^1/_2$ pint/1$^1/_4$ cups vegetable stock
ground black pepper
fresh parsley sprigs, to garnish

1 Peel and cube the pumpkin, place in a small bowl and cover with boiling water. Blanch for 2–3 minutes, then drain and refresh under cold water.

2 Cut the onion into wedges, slice the courgette and plantain and cut the aubergine and red and green peppers into chunks. Trim the mushrooms. Place the vegetables, including the pumpkin, in a large bowl.

3 Mix together the lemon juice, oil, soy sauce, tomato juice, chilli, grated onion, garlic, herbs, cinnamon and black pepper and pour over the vegetables. Toss together and then set aside in a cool place to marinate for a few hours.

4 Thread the vegetables on to eight skewers, using a variety of vegetables on each to make a colourful display. Preheat the grill (broiler).

5 Grill (broil) the vegetables under a low heat for about 15 minutes, turning frequently, until golden brown, basting with the marinade in order to keep the vegetables moist.

6 Place the remaining marinade, butter or margarine and stock in a pan and simmer for 10 minutes to cook the onion and reduce the sauce.

7 Pour the sauce into a serving jug (pitcher) and arrange the vegetable skewers on a plate. Garnish with parsley and serve with a rice dish or salad.

COOK'S TIP
You can use any vegetable that you prefer. Just first parboil any that may require longer cooking.

BLACK-EYED BEAN STEW WITH SPICY PUMPKIN

SERVES 3–4

INGREDIENTS
225g/8oz/1¼ cups black-eyed beans
  (peas), soaked for 4 hours or
  overnight
1 onion, chopped
1 green or red (bell) pepper, seeded
  and chopped
2 garlic cloves, chopped
1 vegetable stock (bouillon) cube
1 thyme sprig or 5ml/1 tsp dried thyme
5ml/1 tsp paprika
2.5ml/½ tsp mixed (apple pie) spice
2 carrots, sliced
15–30ml/1–2 tbsp palm oil
salt and hot pepper sauce

For the spicy pumpkin
675g/1½ lb pumpkin
1 onion
25g/1oz/2 tbsp butter or margarine
2 garlic cloves, crushed
3 tomatoes, peeled and chopped
2.5ml/½ tsp ground cinnamon
10ml/2 tsp curry powder

pinch of grated nutmeg
300ml/½ pint/⅔ cup water
salt, hot pepper sauce and
  ground black pepper

1 Drain the beans, place in a pan and cover generously with water. Bring the beans to the boil.

2 Add the onion, green or red pepper, garlic, stock cube, herbs and spices. Simmer for 45 minutes, or until the beans are just tender. Season to taste with the salt and a little hot pepper sauce.

3 Add the carrots and palm oil and continue cooking for 10–12 minutes, until the carrots are cooked, adding a little more water if necessary. Remove from the heat and set aside.

4 To make the spicy pumpkin, cut the pumpkin into cubes and finely chop the onion.

5 Melt the butter or margarine in a large pan, and add the pumpkin, onion, garlic, tomatoes, spices and water. Stir well to combine and simmer until the pumpkin is soft. Season with salt, hot pepper sauce and black pepper, to taste. Serve with the black-eyed beans.

RED BEAN CHILLI

THIS VEGETARIAN CHILLI CAN BE ADAPTED TO ACCOMMODATE MEAT EATERS BY ADDING EITHER MINCED BEEF OR LAMB IN PLACE OF THE LENTILS. ADD THE MEAT ONCE THE ONIONS ARE SOFT AND FRY UNTIL NICELY BROWNED BEFORE ADDING THE TOMATOES.

SERVES 4

INGREDIENTS
30ml/2 tbsp vegetable oil
1 onion, chopped
400g/14oz can chopped tomatoes
2 garlic cloves, crushed
300ml/½ pint/1¼ cups white wine
about 300ml/½ pint/1¼ cups
  vegetable stock
115g/4oz/½ cup red lentils
2 thyme sprigs or 5ml/1 tsp
  dried thyme
10ml/2 tsp ground cumin
45ml/3 tbsp dark soy sauce
½ hot chilli pepper, finely chopped
5ml/1 tsp mixed (apple pie) spice
15ml/1 tbsp oyster sauce (optional)
225g/8oz can red kidney
  beans, drained
10ml/2 tsp sugar
salt
boiled rice and corn, to serve

1 Heat the oil in a large pan and cook the onion over a medium heat for a few minutes until slightly softened.

2 Add the tomatoes and garlic, cook for 10 minutes, then stir in the wine and vegetable stock.

3 Add the lentils, thyme, cumin, soy sauce, hot pepper, mixed spice and oyster sauce, if using.

4 Cover and simmer for 40 minutes, or until the lentils are cooked, stirring occasionally and adding more water if the lentils begin to dry out.

5 Stir in the kidney beans and sugar and continue cooking for 10 minutes, adding a little extra stock or water if necessary. Season to taste with salt and serve hot with boiled rice and corn.

COOK'S TIP
Fiery chillies can irritate the skin, so always wash your hands well after handling them and take care not to touch your eyes. If you like really hot, spicy food, then add the seeds from the chilli, too.

CHILES RELLENOS

SERVES 4

INGREDIENTS
   8 large green (bell) peppers or fresh
      green chillies such as poblano
   15–30ml/1–2 tbsp vegetable oil, plus
      extra for frying
   450g/1lb/4 cups grated cheese
   4 eggs, separated
   75g/3oz/²⁄₃ cup flour

For the sauce
   15ml/1 tbsp vegetable oil
   1 small onion, chopped
   1.5ml/¼ tsp salt
   5–10ml/1–2 tsp red pepper flakes
   2.5ml/½ tsp ground cumin
   250ml/8fl oz/1 cup beef stock
   750ml/1¼ pints/3 cups canned
      tomatoes

COOK'S TIP
If necessary, work in batches, but do
not coat the (bell) peppers until you are
ready to cook.

1 For the sauce, heat the oil in a frying
pan. Add the onion and cook over a low
heat for 8 minutes, until just soft. Stir in
the salt, pepper flakes, cumin, stock and
tomatoes. Cover and simmer gently for
about 5 minutes, stirring occasionally.

2 Transfer the mixture to a food processor
or blender and process until smooth.
Strain into a clean pan. Taste for
seasoning, and set aside. Preheat the
grill (broiler).

3 Brush the peppers lightly with oil.
Lay them on a baking sheet. Grill (broil)
as close to the heat as possible for
5–8 minutes, until blackened all over.
Cover with a dishtowel and set aside.

4 When cool enough to handle,
remove the charred skin. Carefully slit
the peppers or chillies and scoop out
the seeds.

5 With your hands, form the cheese into
eight cylinders that are slightly shorter than
the peppers. Place the cheese cylinders
inside the peppers. Secure the slits with
cocktail sticks (toothpicks). Set aside.

6 Beat the egg whites until just stiff. Add
the egg yolks, one at a time, beating on
low speed to incorporate them. Beat in
15ml/1 tbsp flour.

7 Put a 2.5cm/1in layer of oil in a frying
pan. Heat until hot but not smoking (to
test, drop a little batter in the oil: if the oil
sizzles, it is hot enough for frying).

8 Coat the peppers lightly in flour all over,
shaking off any excess. Dip into the egg
batter, then place in the hot oil. Fry for
about 2 minutes, until brown on one side.
Turn carefully and brown the other side.

9 Reheat the sauce and serve with the
Chiles Rellenos.

VARIATION
If using (bell) peppers instead of
green chillies, mix the grated cheese
with 15ml/1 tbsp hot chilli powder for
a more authentic south-west taste.

STIR-FRIED CHILLI GREENS

THIS ATTRACTIVE DISH IS SPICED WITH GINGER AND RED CHILLIES, AND GIVEN ADDED ZEST BY THE ADDITION OF OYSTER SAUCE.

SERVES 4

INGREDIENTS

2 bunches spinach or chard or 1 head
  Chinese leaves (Chinese cabbage) or
  450g/1lb curly kale
3 garlic cloves, crushed
5cm/2in fresh root ginger, peeled and
  cut in thin batons
45–60ml/3–4 tbsp groundnut (peanut) oil
115g/4oz boneless, skinless chicken
  breast portion, or pork fillet, or a
  mixture of both, very finely sliced
12 quail's eggs, hard-boiled and
  shelled
1 fresh red chilli, seeded and shredded
30–45ml/2–3 tbsp oyster sauce
15ml/1 tbsp brown sugar
10ml/2 tsp cornflour (cornstarch),
  mixed with 50ml/2fl oz/¼ cup cold
  water
salt

COOK'S TIP
As with all stir-fries, don't start
cooking until you have prepared all
the ingredients and arranged them to
hand. Cut everything into small, even-
size pieces so the food can be cooked
very quickly and all the colours and
flavours preserved.

1 Wash the chosen leaves well and shake them dry. Strip the tender leaves from the stems and tear them into pieces. Discard the lower, tougher part of the stems and slice the remainder evenly.

2 Stir-fry the garlic and ginger in the hot oil, without browning, for 1 minute. Add the chicken and/or pork and keep stirring it in the wok until the meat changes colour. When the meat looks cooked, add the sliced stems first and cook them quickly, then add the torn leaves, quail's eggs and chilli. Spoon in the oyster sauce and a little boiling water, if necessary. Cover and cook for 1–2 minutes only.

3 Remove the cover, stir and add sugar and salt to taste. Stir in the cornflour and water mixture and toss thoroughly. Cook until the mixture is well coated in a glossy sauce.

4 Serve immediately, while still very hot and the colours are bright and positively jewel-like.

GREEN BEAN AND CHILLI PEPPER SALAD

SERVES 4

INGREDIENTS

   350g/12oz/2¼ cups cooked green
     beans, quartered
   2 red (bell) peppers, seeded and
     chopped
   2 spring onions (scallions) (white and
     green parts), chopped
   1 or more drained pickled serrano
     chillies, well rinsed and then seeded
     and chopped
   1 iceberg lettuce, coarsely shredded, or
     mixed salad leaves
   olives, to garnish

For the dressing
   45ml/3 tbsp red wine vinegar
   135ml/9 tbsp olive oil
   salt and ground black pepper

1 Combine the cooked green beans,
chopped peppers, chopped spring onions
and chillies in a salad bowl.

2 Make the salad dressing. Pour the red
wine vinegar into a bowl or jug (pitcher).
Add salt and ground black pepper to
taste, then gradually whisk in the olive oil
until well combined.

3 Pour the salad dressing over the
prepared vegetables and toss lightly
together to mix and coat thoroughly.

4 Line a large platter with the shredded
lettuce leaves and arrange the salad
attractively on top. Garnish with the olives
and serve.

MUSHROOMS WITH CHIPOTLE CHILLIES

SERVES 6

INGREDIENTS
   450g/1lb/4 cups button (white)
     mushrooms
   60ml/4 tbsp olive oil
   1 onion, finely chopped
   2 garlic cloves, chopped
   2 drained canned chipotle chillies,
     rinsed and sliced
   salt
   chopped fresh coriander (cilantro),
     to garnish

COOK'S TIP
Never wash mushrooms as they
quickly absorb water. Wipe them with
kitchen paper or a clean, damp cloth.

1 Wipe the mushrooms gently and carefully with kitchen paper. Heat the olive oil in a large frying pan and add the mushrooms, finely chopped onion, chopped garlic, and sliced chillies. Stir to coat in oil.

2 Cook the mixture over a medium heat for 6–8 minutes, stirring occasionally, until the onions and mushrooms are tender. Season to taste with salt and serve on small individual plates, sprinkled with a little chopped fresh coriander.

JALAPEÑO AND PRAWN SALAD

PICKLED JALAPEÑO CHILLI GIVES A DISTINCTIVE SPICY FLAVOUR TO THIS DELICIOUS SALAD. IN MEXICO, IT IS QUITE USUAL TO SERVE SUCH A HEARTY SALAD AS A SEPARATE COURSE.

SERVES 4

INGREDIENTS
   1 iceberg lettuce or 2 Little Gem
     (Bibb) lettuces, separated into leaves,
     or assorted lettuce leaves
   60ml/4 tbsp mayonnaise
   60ml/4 tbsp sour cream
   350g/12oz/3 cups cooked peeled prawns
     (shrimp), thawed if frozen, chopped
   75g/3oz/1/2 cup cooked green
     beans, chopped
   75g/3oz/1/2 cup cooked
     carrots, chopped
   1/2 cucumber, about 115g/4oz chopped
   2 hard-boiled eggs, coarsely chopped
   1 drained pickled jalapeño chilli, seeded
     and chopped
   salt

1 Line a large salad bowl or platter with the lettuce leaves. Mix the mayonnaise and sour cream together in a small bowl and set aside.

2 Combine the prawns, beans, carrot, cucumber, eggs and chilli in a separate bowl. Season with salt.

3 Add the mayonnaise and sour cream mixture to the prawns, folding it in very gently so that all the ingredients are well mixed and coated with the dressing. Pile the mixture into the lined salad bowl or arrange attractively on the platter. Serve.

SPICY POTATO SALAD

THIS TASTY SALAD IS QUICK TO PREPARE, AND MAKES A SATISFYING ACCOMPANIMENT TO MEAT OR FISH COOKED ON THE BARBECUE.

SERVES 6

INGREDIENTS

900g/2lb potatoes, peeled
2 red (bell) peppers
2 celery sticks
1 shallot
2–3 spring onions (scallions)
1 green chilli, finely chopped
1 garlic clove, crushed
10ml/2 tsp finely chopped
  fresh chives
10ml/2 tsp finely chopped fresh basil
15ml/1 tbsp finely chopped
  fresh parsley
15ml/1 tbsp single (light) cream
30ml/2 tbsp salad cream
15ml/1 tbsp mayonnaise
5ml/1 tsp mild mustard
7.5ml/½ tbsp sugar
chopped fresh chives, to garnish

1 Boil the potatoes until tender but still firm. Drain and cool, then cut into 2.5cm/1in cubes and place in a large salad bowl.

2 Cut the red peppers in half, then cut away and discard the core and seeds and chop the flesh into small pieces. Finely chop the celery, shallot, and spring onions and slice the chilli very thinly, discarding the seeds. Add the vegetables to the potatoes together with the garlic and chopped herbs.

3 Blend the cream, salad cream, mayonnaise, mustard and sugar in a small bowl, stirring until the mixture is well combined.

4 Pour the dressing over the potato and vegetable salad and stir gently to coat evenly. Serve, garnished with the chopped fresh chives.

PEPPERY BEAN SALAD

THIS PRETTY SALAD USES CANNED BEANS FOR SPEED AND CONVENIENCE.

SERVES 4–6

INGREDIENTS
425g/15oz can kidney beans, drained
425g/15oz can black-eyed beans
  (peas), drained
425g/15oz can chickpeas, drained
¼ red (bell) pepper
¼ green (bell) pepper
6 radishes
15ml/1 tbsp chopped spring onion
  (scallion)
5ml/1 tsp ground cumin
15ml/1 tbsp tomato ketchup
30ml/2 tbsp olive oil
15ml/1 tbsp white wine vinegar
1 garlic clove, crushed
½ tsp hot pepper sauce
salt
sliced spring onion, to garnish

COOK'S TIP
For an even tastier salad, allow the
ingredients to marinate for a few hours.

1 Drain the canned beans and chickpeas
and rinse under cold running water.
Shake off the excess water and tip them
into a large salad bowl.

2 Core, seed and chop the peppers. Trim
the radishes and slice thinly. Add to the
beans with the pepper and spring onion.

3 Mix together the cumin, ketchup, oil,
vinegar and garlic in a small bowl. Add a
little salt and hot pepper sauce to taste
and stir again thoroughly.

4 Pour the dressing over the salad and
mix. Chill for at least 1 hour before
serving, garnished with spring onion.

BALTI POTATOES

BALTI IS A TRADITIONAL WAY OF COOKING INDIAN CURRIES IN A KARAHI COOKING PAN.

SERVES 4

INGREDIENTS
75ml/3 tbsp corn oil
2.5ml/¹/₂ tsp white cumin seeds
3 curry leaves
5ml/1 tsp crushed dried red chillies
2.5ml/¹/₂ tsp mixed onion, mustard and
   fenugreek seeds
2.5ml/¹/₂ tsp fennel seeds
3 garlic cloves
2.5ml/¹/₂ tsp shredded ginger
2 onions, sliced
6 new potatoes, sliced thinly
15ml/1 tbsp chopped fresh
   coriander (cilantro)
1 fresh red chilli, seeded and sliced
1 fresh green chilli, seeded and sliced

1 Heat the oil in a deep round-based frying pan or a karahi. Lower the heat slightly and add the cumin seeds, curry leaves, dried red chillies, mixed onion, mustard and fenugreek seeds, fennel seeds, garlic cloves and ginger. Cook for 1 minute, then add the onions and cook for a further 5 minutes, or until the onions are golden brown.

2 Add the potatoes, fresh coriander and fresh red and green chillies and mix together well. Cover the pan tightly with a lid or foil, making sure the foil does not touch the food. Cook over a very low heat for about 7 minutes, or until the potatoes are tender.

3 Remove the pan from the heat, take off the foil and serve hot.

OKRA WITH GREEN MANGO AND LENTILS

IF YOU LIKE OKRA, YOU'LL LOVE THIS SPICY TANGY DISH.

SERVES 4

INGREDIENTS
115g/4oz/¹/₂ cup yellow lentils
45ml/3 tbsp corn oil
2.5ml/¹/₂ tsp onion seeds
2 onions, sliced
2.5ml/¹/₂ tsp ground fenugreek
5ml/1 tsp ginger pulp
5ml/1 tsp garlic pulp
7.5ml/1¹/₂ tsp chilli powder
1.5ml/¹/₄ tsp ground turmeric
5ml/1 tsp ground coriander
1 green mango, peeled and sliced
450g/1lb okra, cut into
   1cm/¹/₂in pieces
7.5ml/1¹/₂ tsp salt
2 fresh red chillies, seeded and sliced
30ml/2 tbsp chopped fresh
   coriander (cilantro)
1 tomato, sliced

1 Wash the lentils thoroughly and put in a pan with enough water to cover. Bring to the boil and cook until soft but not mushy. Drain and set to one side.

2 Heat the oil in a deep round-based frying pan or a karahi and cook the onion seeds until they begin to pop. Add the onions and cook until golden brown. Lower the heat and add the ground fenugreek, ginger, garlic, chilli powder, turmeric and ground coriander.

3 Throw in the mango slices and the okra. Stir well and add the salt, red chillies and fresh coriander. Stir-fry for approximately 3 minutes, or until the okra is well cooked.

4 Finally, add the cooked lentils and sliced tomato and cook for a further 3 minutes. Serve hot.

SPICY VEGETABLES WITH ALMONDS

<u>SERVES 4</u>

INGREDIENTS

30ml/2 tbsp vegetable oil
2 onions, sliced
5cm/2in fresh root ginger, shredded
5ml/1 tsp crushed black peppercorns
1 bay leaf
1.5ml/¼ tsp ground turmeric
5ml/1 tsp ground coriander
5ml/1 tsp salt
2.5ml/½ tsp garam masala
175g/6oz/2½ cups mushrooms, sliced
1 courgette (zucchini), thickly sliced
50g/2oz/⅓ cup green beans, sliced
   into 2.5cm/1in pieces
15ml/1 tbsp chopped fresh mint
150ml/¼ pint/⅔ cup water
30ml/2 tbsp natural (plain) yogurt
25g/1oz/¼ cup flaked (sliced) almonds

1 In a medium deep frying pan, heat the vegetable oil and cook the sliced onions with the shredded fresh ginger, crushed black peppercorns and the bay leaf for 3–5 minutes.

2 Lower the heat and add the turmeric, ground coriander, salt and garam masala, stirring occasionally. Gradually add the mushrooms, courgette, green beans and the mint. Stir gently so that the vegetables retain their shape.

3 Pour in the water and bring to a simmer, then lower the heat and cook until most of the water has evaporated.

4 Beat the natural yogurt well with a fork, then pour it on to the vegetables in the pan and mix together well.

5 Cook the spicy vegetables for a further 2–3 minutes, stirring occasionally. Sprinkle with flaked almonds and serve.

COOK'S TIP
For an extra creamy dish, use sour cream instead of the yogurt.

MASALA BEANS WITH FENUGREEK

"MASALA" MEANS SPICE AND THIS VEGETARIAN DISH IS SPICY, ALTHOUGH NOT NECESSARILY HOT. YOU CAN ADAPT THE SPICINESS OF THE DISH BY USING SMALLER OR LARGER QUANTITIES OF THE SPICES, AS YOU WISH. SERVE IT AS AN ACCOMPANIMENT TO A MEAT DISH WITH FRESHLY COOKED BASMATI RICE FOR A WONDERFUL INDIAN MEAL.

SERVES 4

INGREDIENTS

1 onion
5ml/1 tsp ground cumin
5ml/1 tsp ground coriander
5ml/1 tsp sesame seeds
5ml/1 tsp chilli powder
2.5ml/1/2 tsp garlic pulp
1.5ml/1/4 tsp ground turmeric
5ml/1 tsp salt
30ml/2 tbsp vegetable oil
1 tomato, quartered
225g/8oz/1 1/2 cups green beans
1 bunch fresh fenugreek leaves,
 stems discarded
60ml/4 tbsp chopped coriander (cilantro)
15ml/1 tbsp lemon juice

1 Coarsely chop the onion. In a mixing bowl, combine the ground cumin and coriander, sesame seeds, chilli powder, garlic pulp, turmeric and salt. Mix well.

2 Place all of these ingredients, including the onion, in a food processor or blender and process for 30–45 seconds.

3 In a medium pan, heat the vegetable oil and cook the spice mixture for about 5 minutes, stirring occasionally as the mixture cooks.

4 Add the quartered tomato, green beans, fresh fenugreek and fresh chopped coriander.

5 Stir-fry the mixture for about 5 minutes, then sprinkle over the lemon juice, pour into a serving dish and serve immediately.

COOK'S TIP
If you can't find fenugreek leaves, use 5ml/1 tsp fenugreek seeds instead.

Rice and noodles are the cornerstones of many

cuisines and their unassertive taste lends itself to

flavouring with mild or hot spices, or a mixture of

both. Many of the classic rice dishes appear: Nasi

Goreng, Chicken Jambalaya and Sushi, seasoned

with the breathtaking wasabi paste. Noodle dishes

are justly popular in Thailand and China where

they are combined with chillies, limes, sesame oil,

coriander and many other emphatic ingredients to

produce such delights as Spicy Sichuan Noodles and

Thai Fried Noodles.

Flame-filled Rice and Noodles

YOGURT CHICKEN AND RICE

THIS IS FLAVOURED WITH ZERESHK, SMALL DRIED BERRIES AVAILABLE FROM MIDDLE EASTERN STORES.

SERVES 6

INGREDIENTS
40g/1½oz/3 tbsp butter
1.5kg/3–3½lb chicken pieces
1 large onion, chopped
250ml/8fl oz/1 cup chicken stock
2 eggs
475ml/16fl oz/2 cups natural
 (plain) yogurt
2–3 saffron threads, dissolved in
 15ml/1 tbsp boiling water
5ml/1 tsp ground cinnamon
450g/1lb/generous 2¼ cups basmati
 rice, soaked in salted water for
 2 hours
75g/3oz/⅓ cup zereshk
salt and ground black pepper
herb salad, to serve

1 Melt two-thirds of the butter in a casserole and cook the chicken and onion for 4–5 minutes, until the onion is softened and the chicken browned.

2 Add the stock and salt and pepper, bring to the boil and then simmer for 45 minutes, or until the chicken is cooked and the stock reduced by half.

3 Skin and bone the chicken. Cut the flesh into large pieces and place in a large bowl. Reserve the stock.

4 Beat the eggs and blend with the yogurt. Add the saffron water and cinnamon and season with salt and pepper. Pour over the chicken and leave to marinate on one side for up to 2 hours.

5 Drain the rice and then boil in salted water for 5 minutes, reduce the heat and simmer very gently for 10 minutes, until half cooked. Drain and rinse in warm water.

6 Transfer the chicken from the yogurt mixture to a dish and mix half the rice into the yogurt.

7 Preheat the oven to 160°C/325°F/Gas 3 and grease a large 10cm/4in deep ovenproof dish.

8 Place the rice and yogurt mixture in the base of the dish, arrange the chicken pieces in a layer on top and then add the plain rice. Warm the zereshk thoroughly, then sprinkle over.

9 Mix the remaining butter with the chicken stock and pour over the rice. Cover tightly with foil and cook in the oven for 35–45 minutes.

10 Leave the dish to cool for a few minutes. Place on a cold, damp dishtowel, which will help lift the rice from the base of the dish, then run a knife around the inside edge of the dish. Place a large flat plate over the dish and turn out. You should have a rice "cake" which can be cut into wedges. Serve hot with a herb salad.

LOUISIANA RICE

AUBERGINE AND PORK COMBINE WITH HERBS AND SPICES TO MAKE A HIGHLY FLAVOURSOME DISH.

<u>SERVES 4</u>

INGREDIENTS

60ml/4 tbsp vegetable oil
1 small aubergine (eggplant), diced
225g/8oz/2 cups minced (ground) pork
1 green (bell) pepper, seeded and chopped
2 celery sticks, chopped
1 onion, chopped
1 garlic clove, crushed
5ml/1 tsp cayenne pepper
5ml/1 tsp paprika
5ml/1 tsp black pepper
2.5ml/$\frac{1}{2}$ tsp salt
5ml/1 tsp dried thyme
2.5ml/$\frac{1}{2}$ tsp dried oregano
475ml/16fl oz/2 cups chicken stock
225g/8oz chicken livers, minced
  (ground)
150g/5oz/scant $\frac{2}{3}$ cup long grain rice
1 bay leaf
45ml/3 tbsp chopped fresh parsley
celery leaves, to garnish

1 Heat the oil in a frying pan until piping hot, then add the aubergine and stir-fry for about 5 minutes.

2 Add the pork and cook for 6–8 minutes, until browned, using a wooden spoon to break up any lumps.

3 Add the green pepper, celery, onion, garlic and all the spices and herbs. Cover and cook over a high heat for 5–6 minutes, stirring frequently from the base of the pan to scrape up and distribute the crispy brown bits.

4 Pour in the chicken stock and stir to remove any sediment from the base of the pan. Cover and cook for 6 minutes over a medium heat. Stir in the chicken livers, cook for 2 minutes, then stir in the rice and add the bay leaf.

5 Reduce the heat, cover and simmer for 6–7 minutes. Turn off the heat and leave to stand for 10–15 minutes until the rice is tender. Remove the bay leaf and stir in the chopped parsley. Serve the rice hot, garnished with the celery leaves.

SPICY FISH AND RICE

THIS ARABIC FISH DISH, SAYADICH IS ESPECIALLY POPULAR IN LEBANON.

SERVES 4–6

INGREDIENTS
   juice of 1 lemon
   45ml/3 tbsp oil
   900g/2lb cod steaks
   4 large onions, chopped
   5ml/1 tsp ground cumin
   2–3 saffron threads
   1 litre/1³/4 pints/4 cups fish stock
   450g/1lb/generous 2¹/4 cups basmati
      or long grain rice
   50g/2oz/¹/2 cup pine nuts,
      lightly toasted
   salt and ground black pepper
   fresh parsley, to garnish

1 Blend the lemon juice and 15ml/
1 tbsp of oil in a shallow dish. Add the
fish, turn to coat thoroughly, then cover
and marinate for 30 minutes.

2 Heat the remaining oil in a large pan
and cook the onions for approximately
5–6 minutes, stirring occasionally.

3 Drain the fish, reserving the
marinade, and add to the pan. Cook for
1–2 minutes each side, until lightly
golden, then add the cumin, saffron
threads and a little salt and pepper.

4 Pour in the fish stock and the reserved
marinade, bring to the boil and then
simmer for 5–10 minutes, or until the fish
is nearly done.

5 Transfer the fish to a plate and add the
rice to the stock. Bring to the boil, reduce
the heat and simmer gently for 15
minutes, until nearly all the stock has
been absorbed.

6 Arrange the fish on top of the rice and
cover the pan. Steam over a low heat for
15–20 minutes.

7 Transfer the fish to a plate, spoon the
rice on to a large flat dish and arrange
the fish on top. Sprinkle with toasted pine
nuts and garnish with fresh parsley.

MASALA PRAWNS AND RICE

SERVES 4–6

INGREDIENTS
   2 large onions, sliced and deep-fried
   300ml/¹/2 pint/1¹/4 cups natural
      (plain) yogurt
   30ml/2 tbsp tomato purée (paste)
   60ml/4 tbsp green masala paste
   30ml/2 tbsp lemon juice
   5ml/1 tsp black cumin seeds
   5cm/2in cinnamon stick
   4 green cardamom pods
   450g/1lb fresh king prawns (jumbo
      shrimp), peeled and deveined
   225g/8oz/3 cups button (white) mushrooms
   225g/8oz/2 cups frozen peas, thawed
   450g/1lb/generous 2¹/4 cups basmati
      rice soaked for 5 minutes in boiled
      water and drained
   300ml/¹/2 pint/1¹/4 cups water
   1 sachet saffron powder mixed in
      90ml/6 tbsp milk
   30ml/2 tbsp ghee or unsalted (sweet) butter
   salt

1 Mix the first 8 ingredients together with
salt to taste. Mix the prawns, mushrooms
and peas into the marinade and leave for
about 2 hours.

2 Grease the base of a heavy pan and
add the prawns, vegetables and any
marinade juices. Cover with the
drained rice and smooth the surface
gently until you have an even layer.

3 Pour the water all over the surface of
the rice. Make random holes through the
rice with the handle of a spoon and pour
in the saffron milk.

4 Dot the ghee or butter on the surface
and place a circular piece of foil directly
on top of the rice. Cover and steam over
a low heat for 45–50 minutes, until the
rice is cooked Gently toss the rice,
prawns and vegetables together and
serve hot.

SPICED TROUT PILAFF

SMOKED TROUT MIGHT SEEM AN UNUSUAL PARTNER FOR RICE, BUT THIS IS A WINNING COMBINATION.

SERVES 4

INGREDIENTS

225g/8oz/generous 1 cup basmati rice
40g/1½ oz/3 tbsp butter
2 onions, sliced into rings
1 garlic clove, crushed
2 bay leaves
2 whole cloves
2 green cardamom pods
2.5cm/2in cinnamon sticks
5ml/1 tsp cumin seeds
4 hot-smoked trout fillets, skinned
50g/2oz/½ cup slivered (sliced)
   almonds, toasted
50g/2oz/scant ½ cup seedless raisins
30ml/2 tbsp chopped fresh parsley
mango chutney and poppadums,
   to serve

1 Wash the rice thoroughly in several changes of water and drain well. Set aside. Melt the butter in a large frying pan and cook the onions until well browned, stirring frequently.

2 Add the garlic, bay leaves, cloves, cardamom pods, cinnamon and cumin seeds and stir-fry for 1 minute.

3 Stir in the rice, then add 600ml/ 1 pint/2½ cups boiling water. Bring to the boil. Cover the pan tightly, reduce the heat and cook very gently for 20–25 minutes, until the water has been absorbed and the rice is tender.

4 Flake the smoked trout and add to the pan with the almonds and raisins. Fork through gently. Cover the pan and allow the smoked trout to warm in the rice for a few minutes. Sprinkle over the parsley and serve with mango chutney and poppadums.

NASI GORENG

ONE OF THE MOST POPULAR AND BEST-KNOWN INDONESIAN DISHES, THIS IS A MARVELLOUS WAY TO USE UP LEFTOVER RICE, CHICKEN AND MEATS SUCH AS PORK.

SERVES 4–6

INGREDIENTS

350g/12oz/scant 1¹/2 cups dry weight
    basmati rice, cooked and cooled
2 eggs
30ml/2 tbsp water
105ml/7 tbsp oil
225g/8oz pork fillet (tenderloin) or
    fillet (tenderloin) of beef
2–3 fresh red chillies, seeded and sliced
1cm/¹/2 in cube shrimp paste
2 garlic cloves, crushed
1 onion, sliced
115g/4oz/1 cup cooked, peeled prawns
225g/8oz/1¹/2 cups cooked chicken,
    chopped
30ml/2 tbsp dark soy sauce or
    45–60ml/3–4 tbsp tomato ketchup
salt and ground black pepper
celery leaves, deep-fried onions and
    coriander (cilantro) sprigs, to garnish

1 Separate the grains of the cooked and cooled rice with a fork. Cover and set aside until needed.

2 Beat the eggs with the water and season lightly. Make two or three thin omelettes in a frying pan, with a minimum of oil and leave to cool. When cold, roll up each omelette and cut into strips. Set aside.

3 Cut the pork or beef fillet into neat strips. Finely shred one of the chillies and set aside.

4 Put the shrimp paste with the remaining chilli, the garlic and onion, in a food processor, or use a mortar and pestle, and grind to a fine paste.

5 Heat the remaining oil in a wok and stir-fry the paste, without browning, until it gives off a rich, spicy aroma. Add the pork or beef, tossing the meat all the time to seal in the juices. Cook for 2 minutes, stirring constantly. Add the prawns, cook for 2 minutes and then stir in the chicken, cold rice, dark soy sauce or ketchup and season to taste. Stir all the time to keep the rice light and fluffy and prevent it from sticking.

6 Turn on to a hot serving plate and garnish with the omelette strips, celery leaves, onions, reserved shredded chilli and the coriander sprigs.

SEAFOOD AND RICE

INGREDIENTS
    30ml/2 tbsp oil
    115g/4oz smoked bacon, rind
      removed, diced
    1 onion, chopped
    2 celery sticks, chopped
    2 large garlic cloves, chopped
    10ml/2 tsp cayenne pepper
    2 bay leaves
    5ml/1 tsp dried oregano
    2.5ml/$^{1}/_{2}$ tsp dried thyme
    4 tomatoes, peeled and chopped
    150ml/$^{1}/_{4}$ pint/$^{2}/_{3}$ cup tomato sauce
    350g/12oz/1$^{3}/_{4}$ cups long grain rice
    475ml/16fl oz/2 cups fish stock
    175g/6oz cod, or haddock, skinned,
      boned and cubed
    115g/4oz/1 cup cooked, peeled
      prawns (shrimp)
    salt and ground black pepper
    2 spring onions (scallions), chopped,
      to garnish

1 Preheat the oven to 180°C/350°F/Gas 4. Heat the oil in a large pan and fry the bacon until crisp. Add the onion and celery and stir until beginning to stick to the pan.

2 Add the garlic, cayenne pepper, herbs, tomatoes and seasoning and mix well. Stir in the tomato sauce, rice and stock and bring to the boil.

3 Gently stir in the fish and transfer to an ovenproof dish. Cover tightly with foil and bake for 20–30 minutes, until the rice is just tender. Stir in the prawns and heat through. Serve sprinkled with the spring onions.

CHICKEN JAMBALAYA

INGREDIENTS
    2 × 1.5kg/3–3$^{1}/_{2}$ lb chickens
    450g/1lb raw smoked gammon
      (cured ham)
    50g/2oz/4 tbsp lard or bacon fat
    50g/2oz/$^{1}/_{2}$ cup plain (all-purpose) flour
    3 onions, finely sliced
    2 green (bell) peppers, seeded and
      sliced
    675g/1$^{1}/_{2}$ lb tomatoes, chopped
    2–3 garlic cloves, crushed
    10ml/2 tsp chopped fresh thyme or
      5ml/1 tsp dried thyme
    24 Mediterranean prawns (shrimp),
      peeled
    500g/1$^{1}/_{4}$ lb/scant 3 cups long
      grain rice
    2–3 dashes Tabasco sauce
    6 spring onions (scallions), finely chopped
    45ml/3 tbsp chopped fresh parsley
    salt and ground black pepper

1 Cut each chicken into 10 pieces and season. Dice the gammon, discarding the rind and fat.

2 In a large casserole, melt the lard or bacon fat and brown the chicken pieces all over, lifting them out and setting them aside as they are done.

3 Turn the heat down, sprinkle the flour on to the fat in the pan and stir until the roux turns golden brown.

4 Return the chicken pieces to the pan, add the diced gammon, onions, green peppers, tomatoes, garlic and thyme and cook, stirring regularly, for 10 minutes, then stir in the prawns.

5 Stir the rice into the pan with one-and-a-half times the rice's volume in cold water. Season with salt, pepper and Tabasco sauce. Bring to the boil and cook over a low heat until the rice is tender and the liquid absorbed. Add a little extra boiling water if the rice dries out before it is cooked.

6 Mix the spring onions and parsley into the finished dish, reserving a little of the mixture to sprinkle over the jambalaya. Serve hot.

SPICY RICE CAKES

MAKES 16 CAKES

INGREDIENTS

1 garlic clove, crushed
1cm/½ in piece fresh root ginger,
   peeled and finely chopped
1.5ml/¼ tsp ground turmeric
5ml/1 tsp sugar
2.5ml/½ tsp salt
5ml/1 tsp chilli sauce
10ml/2 tsp fish or soy sauce
30ml/2 tbsp chopped fresh
   coriander (cilantro)
juice of ½ lime
115g/4oz/generous ½ cup dry weight
   long grain rice, cooked
peanuts, chopped
150ml/¼ pint/⅔ cup vegetable oil, for
   deep-frying
coriander sprigs, to garnish

1 In a food processor, process the garlic, ginger and turmeric. Add the sugar, salt, chilli and fish or soy sauce, coriander and lime juice.

2 Add three-quarters of the cooked rice and process until smooth and sticky. Transfer to a mixing bowl and stir in the remainder of the rice. Wet your hands and shape into thumb-size balls.

3 Roll the balls in chopped peanuts to coat evenly. Then set aside until ready to cook and serve.

4 Heat the vegetable oil in a deep frying pan. Prepare a tray lined with kitchen paper to drain the rice cakes. Deep-fry three cakes at a time until crisp and golden, remove with a slotted spoon, then drain on the kitchen paper before serving hot.

RED RICE RISSOLES

SERVES 6

INGREDIENTS

1 large red onion, chopped
1 red (bell) pepper, chopped
2 garlic cloves, crushed
1 red chilli, finely chopped
30ml/2 tbsp olive oil
25g/1oz/2 tbsp butter
225g/8oz/generous 1 cup risotto rice
1 litre/1¾ pints/4 cups stock
4 sun-dried tomatoes, chopped
30ml/2 tbsp tomato purée (paste)
10ml/2 tsp dried oregano
45ml/3 tbsp chopped fresh parsley
150g/6oz cheese, e.g. red Leicester or
   smoked Cheddar
1 egg, beaten
115g/4oz/1 cup dried breadcrumbs
oil, for deep-frying
salt and ground black pepper

1 Cook the onion, pepper, garlic and chilli in the oil and butter for 5 minutes. Stir in the rice and cook for a further 2 minutes.

2 Pour in the stock and add the sun-dried tomatoes, purée, oregano and seasoning. Bring to the boil, stirring occasionally, then cover and simmer for 20 minutes.

3 Stir in the parsley, then turn into a shallow dish and chill until firm. When cold, divide into 12 and shape into equal-sized balls.

4 Cut the cheese into 12 pieces and press a nugget into the centre of each rice rissole.

5 Put the beaten egg in one bowl and the breadcrumbs into another. Dip the rissoles first into the egg, then into the breadcrumbs, coating each of them evenly and completely.

6 Place the rissoles on a plate and chill again for 30 minutes. Fill a deep frying pan one-third full of oil and heat until a cube of day-old bread browns in less than a minute.

7 Fry the rissoles, in batches, for about 3–4 minutes, reheating the oil in between. Drain on kitchen paper and keep warm, uncovered. Serve with a side salad.

PERSIAN RICE WITH A TAHDEEG

PERSIAN OR IRANIAN CUISINE IS EXOTIC AND DELICIOUS, AND THE FLAVOURS ARE INTENSE. A TAHDEEG IS THE GLORIOUS, GOLDEN RICE CRUST OR "DIG" THAT FORMS ON THE BASE OF THE PAN.

SERVES 8

INGREDIENTS

   450g/1lb/generous 2¼ cups basmati
     rice, rinsed thoroughly and soaked
   2 garlic cloves, crushed
   2 onions, 1 chopped, 1 thinly sliced
   150ml/¼ pint/²/₃ cup sunflower oil
   150g/5oz/²/₃ cup green lentils, soaked
   600ml/1 pint/2½ cups stock
   50g/2oz/½ cup raisins
   10ml/2 tsp ground coriander
   45ml/3 tbsp tomato purée (paste)
   a few saffron threads
   1 egg yolk, beaten
   10ml/2 tsp natural (plain) yogurt
   75g/3oz/6 tbsp butter, melted
     and strained
   extra oil, for frying
   salt and ground black pepper

1 Drain the soaked rice, then cook it in plenty of boiling salted water for 10–12 minutes or until tender. Drain again.

2 In a large pan, cook the garlic and chopped onion in 30ml/2 tbsp oil for 5 minutes.

3 Add the lentils, stock, raisins, coriander, tomato purée and seasoning to the pan. Bring to the boil, then cover and simmer for 20 minutes.

4 Soak the saffron threads in a little hot water. Remove about 120ml/8 tbsp of the cooked rice and mix with the egg yolk and yogurt. Season well.

5 In a large pan, heat about two-thirds of the remaining oil and sprinkle the egg and yogurt rice evenly over the base.

6 Sprinkle the remaining rice into the pan, alternating it with the lentil mixture. Build up in a pyramid shape away from the sides of the pan, finishing with plain rice on top.

7 With a long wooden spoon handle, make three holes down to the base of the pan and drizzle over the butter. Bring to a high heat, then wrap the pan lid in a clean, wet dishtowel and place firmly on top. When a good head of steam appears, turn the heat down to low. Cook for about 30 minutes.

8 Meanwhile, cook the sliced onion in the remaining oil until browned and crisp. Drain well and set aside.

9 Remove the rice pan from the heat, still covered, and stand it briefly in a sink of cold water for 1–2 minutes to loosen the base. Remove the lid and mix a few spoons of the white rice with the saffron water.

10 Toss the rice and lentils together in the pan. Spoon on to a large serving dish. Sprinkle the saffron rice on top. Break up the rice crust on the pan base and place pieces of it around the mound. Sprinkle over the crispy fried onions and serve.

FESTIVE RICE

THIS THAI DISH IS TRADITIONALLY SERVED SHAPED INTO A CONE AND SURROUNDED BY A VARIETY OF ACCOMPANIMENTS.

SERVES 8

INGREDIENTS
450g/1lb/generous 2¼ cups Thai
   fragrant rice
60ml/4 tbsp oil
2 garlic cloves, crushed
2 onions, finely sliced
5cm/2in fresh turmeric, peeled
   and crushed
750ml/1¼ pints/3 cups water
400ml/14fl oz can coconut milk
1–2 lemon grass stalks, bruised

For the accompaniments
   omelette strips
   2 fresh red chillies, shredded
   cucumber chunks
   tomato wedges
   deep-fried onions
   prawn (shrimp) crackers

1 Wash the rice in several changes of water. Drain well.

2 Heat the oil in a wok and gently cook the garlic, onions and turmeric for a few minutes, until softened but not browned.

3 Add the rice and stir well so that each grain is thoroughly coated. Pour in the water and coconut milk and add the lemon grass.

4 Bring to the boil, stirring well. Cover the pan and cook gently for 15–20 minutes, or until the liquid is completely absorbed.

5 Remove the pan from the heat. Cover with a clean dishtowel, put on the lid and leave to stand in a warm place for about 15 minutes.

6 Remove the lemon grass, turn out on to a serving platter and garnish the dish with the accompaniments.

INDIAN PILAU RICE

SERVES 4

INGREDIENTS

225g/8oz/generous 1 cup basmati
  rice, rinsed well
30ml/2 tbsp vegetable oil
1 small onion, finely chopped
1 garlic clove, crushed
5ml/1 tsp fennel seeds
15ml/1 tbsp sesame seeds
2.5ml/$\frac{1}{2}$ tsp ground turmeric
5ml/1 tsp ground cumin
1.5ml/$\frac{1}{2}$ tsp salt
2 whole cloves
4 green cardamom pods, lightly
  crushed
5 black peppercorns
450ml/$\frac{3}{4}$ pint/scant 2 cups
  vegetable stock
15ml/1 tbsp ground almonds
coriander (cilantro) sprigs, to garnish

1 Soak the rice in water for 30 minutes. Heat the oil in a pan, add the onion and garlic, and cook gently for 5–6 minutes, until softened.

2 Stir in the fennel and sesame seeds, the turmeric, cumin, salt, cloves, cardamom pods and peppercorns and cook for about 1 minute. Drain the rice well, add it to the pan and stir-fry for a further 3 minutes.

3 Pour in the vegetable stock. Bring to the boil, then cover, reduce the heat to very low and simmer gently for 20 minutes, without removing the lid, until all the liquid has been absorbed.

4 Remove from the heat and leave to stand for 2–3 minutes. Fork up the rice and stir in the ground almonds. Garnish the rice with coriander sprigs.

OKRA FRIED RICE

Sliced okra provides a wonderful creamy texture to this delicious, simple dish.

SERVES 3–4

INGREDIENTS

30ml/2 tbsp vegetable oil
15ml/1 tbsp butter or margarine
1 garlic clove, crushed
$\frac{1}{2}$ red onion, finely chopped
115g/4oz okra, trimmed
30ml/2 tbsp diced green and red
  (bell) peppers
2.5ml/$\frac{1}{2}$ tsp dried thyme
2 green chillies, finely chopped
2.5ml/$\frac{1}{2}$ tsp five-spice powder
1 vegetable stock (bouillon) cube
30ml/2 tbsp soy sauce
15ml/1 tbsp chopped coriander
  (cilantro)
225g/8oz/3 cups cooked rice
salt and ground black pepper
coriander sprigs, to garnish

1 Heat the oil and the butter or margarine in a frying pan, add the garlic and onion and cook over a medium heat for about 5 minutes, until soft.

2 Thinly slice the okra, add to the frying pan and stir-fry gently for a further 6–7 minutes.

3 Add the green and red peppers, thyme, chillies and five-spice powder and cook for 3 minutes. Crumble in the stock cube.

4 Add the soy sauce, coriander and rice and heat through, stirring. Season with salt and pepper. Serve hot, garnished with coriander sprigs.

PISTACHIO PILAFF

SAFFRON AND GINGER ARE TRADITIONAL RICE SPICES AND DELICIOUS WHEN MIXED WITH FRESH PISTACHIOS.

SERVES 4

INGREDIENTS

3 onions
60ml/4 tbsp olive oil
2 garlic cloves, crushed
2.5cm/1in piece fresh root
　ginger, grated
1 green chilli, chopped
2 carrots, coarsely grated
225g/8oz/generous 1 cup basmati
　rice, rinsed
1.5ml/$\frac{1}{4}$ tsp saffron threads, crushed
450ml/$\frac{3}{4}$ pint/scant 2 cups stock
5cm/2in cinnamon stick
5ml/1 tsp ground coriander
75g/3oz/$\frac{3}{4}$ cup fresh pistachios
450g/1lb fresh leaf spinach
5ml/1 tsp garam masala
salt and ground black pepper
tomato salad, to serve

1 Coarsely chop two of the onions. Heat half the oil in a large pan and cook the chopped onions with half the garlic, the ginger and the chilli for 5 minutes, until they are softened.

2 Mix in the carrots and rice, cook for 1 more minute and then add the saffron, stock, cinnamon and coriander. Season well. Bring to the boil, then cover and simmer gently for 10 minutes without lifting the lid.

3 Remove from the heat and leave to stand, uncovered, for 5 minutes. Add the pistachios, mixing them in with a fork. Remove the cinnamon stick and keep the rice warm.

4 Thinly slice the third onion and cook in the remaining oil for about 3 minutes. Stir in the spinach. Cover and cook for another 2 minutes.

5 Add the garam masala powder. Cook until just tender, then drain and coarsely chop the spinach.

6 Spoon the spinach around the edge of a round serving dish and pile the pilaff in the centre. Serve immediately with a tomato salad.

BASMATI AND NUT PILAFF

USE WHATEVER NUTS ARE YOUR FAVOURITE IN THIS DISH — EVEN UNSALTED PEANUTS ARE GOOD, ALTHOUGH ALMONDS, CASHEW NUTS OR PISTACHIOS ARE MORE EXOTIC.

SERVES 4–6

INGREDIENTS

225g/8oz/generous 1 cup basmati rice
1 onion, chopped
1 garlic clove, crushed
1 large carrot, coarsely grated
15–30ml/1–2 tbsp sunflower oil
5ml/1 tsp cumin seeds
10ml/2 tsp ground coriander
10ml/2 tsp black mustard seeds
   (optional)
4 green cardamom pods
450ml/³/₄ pint/scant 2 cups stock
   or water
1 bay leaf
75g/3oz/³/₄ cup unsalted nuts
salt and ground black pepper
fresh chopped parsley or coriander
   (cilantro), to garnish

1 Wash the rice in a sieve under cold running water. If there is time, soak the rice for 30 minutes, then drain it well using a sieve.

2 In a large shallow frying pan, gently cook the onion, garlic and carrot in the oil for 3–4 minutes.

3 Stir in the rice and spices and cook for a further 1–2 minutes so that the grains are coated in oil.

4 Pour in the stock or water, add the bay leaf and season well. Bring to the boil, cover and simmer very gently.

5 Remove from the heat without lifting the lid. Leave to stand on one side for about 5 minutes.

6 If the rice is cooked, there will be small steam holes in the centre of the pan. Discard the bay leaf and cardamom pods.

7 Stir in the nuts and check the seasoning. Sprinkle over the chopped parsley or coriander.

COCONUT RICE

THIS IS A VERY POPULAR WAY OF COOKING RICE THROUGHOUT THE WHOLE OF SOUTH-EAST ASIA. NASI UDUK MAKES A WONDERFUL ACCOMPANIMENT TO ANY DISH, AND GOES PARTICULARLY WELL WITH FISH, CHICKEN AND PORK.

SERVES 4–6

INGREDIENTS
   350g/12oz/1³/₄ cups Thai fragrant rice
   400ml/14fl oz can coconut milk
   300ml/¹/₂ pint/1¹/₄ cups water
   2.5ml/¹/₂ tsp ground coriander
   1 cinnamon stick
   1 lemon grass stalk, bruised
   1 *pandan* or bay leaf (optional)
   salt
   deep-fried onions, to garnish

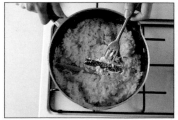

1 Wash the rice in several changes of water then put in a pan with the coconut milk, water, coriander, cinnamon stick, lemon grass and *pandan* or bay leaf, if using, and salt. Bring to the boil, stirring to prevent the rice from settling on the base of the pan. Cover and cook over a very low heat for 12–15 minutes, or until all the coconut milk has been absorbed.

2 Fork the rice through carefully and remove the cinnamon stick, lemon grass and *pandan* or bay leaf. Cover the pan with a tight-fitting lid then cook over the lowest possible heat for 3–5 minutes.

3 Pile the rice on to a warm serving dish and serve garnished with the crisp deep-fried onions.

SPICY RICE WITH CHICKEN

THIS IS A DISH THAT IS POPULAR ALL OVER THE EAST, IN COUNTRIES SUCH AS INDONESIA. IT IS OFTEN SERVED AS SUSTAINING BREAKFAST FARE. HEARTY EATERS TUCK INTO A FEAST OF SPICY RICE WITH CHICKEN, AND ADD PRAWNS, DEEP-FRIED ONIONS, GARLIC AND STRIPS OF FRESH RED AND GREEN CHILLI. THIS IS TOPPED WITH A LIGHTLY FRIED EGG AND GARNISHED WITH CELERY LEAVES.

SERVES 6

INGREDIENTS
   1kg/2¹/₄ lb chicken, cut in 4 pieces or
     4 chicken quarters
   1.75 litres/3 pints/7¹/₂ cups water
   1 large onion, quartered
   2.5cm/1in fresh root ginger, peeled,
     halved and bruised
   350g/12oz/1³/₄ cups Thai fragrant
     rice, rinsed
   salt and ground black pepper

3 Add the rinsed rice to the chicken stock and stir constantly until it comes to the boil, to prevent the rice from settling on the base of the pan. Simmer gently for 20 minutes, without a lid. Stir, cover and cook for a further 20 minutes, stirring occasionally, until the rice is soft and rather like a creamy risotto.

1 Place the chicken pieces in a large pan with the water, onion quarters and ginger. Add seasoning to taste, bring to the boil and simmer for 45–50 minutes, until the chicken is tender. Remove from the heat. Lift out the chicken, remove the meat and discard the skin and bones. Cut the chicken into bite-size pieces. Reserve the stock.

2 Strain the chicken stock into a clean pan and make it up to 1.75 litres/ 3 pints/7¹/₂ cups with water.

4 Stir the chicken pieces into the mixture and heat through for 5 minutes. Serve as it is, or with any of the accompaniments suggested in the introduction.

SUSHI

MAKES 8–10

INGREDIENTS

Tuna sushi

    3 sheets nori (paper-thin seaweed)
    150g/5oz fresh tuna fillet, cut
        into sticks
    5ml/1 tsp wasabi (Japanese horseradish)
    6 young carrots, blanched
    450g/1lb/6 cups cooked Japanese rice

Salmon sushi

    2 eggs
    2.5ml/$^1/_2$ tsp salt
    10ml/2 tsp sugar
    5 sheets nori
    450g/1lb/6 cups cooked Japanese rice
    150g/5oz fresh salmon fillet, cut
        into sticks
    5ml/1 tsp wasabi paste
    $^1/_2$ small cucumber, cut into strips

1 To make the tuna sushi, spread half a sheet of nori on to a bamboo mat, lay strips of tuna across the full length and season with the thinned wasabi. Place a line of blanched carrot next to the tuna and roll tightly. Moisten the edge with water and seal.

2 Place a square of damp wax paper on to the bamboo mat, then spread evenly with sushi rice. Place the non-wrapped tuna along the centre and wrap tightly, enclosing the nori completely. Remove the paper and cut into neat rounds using a wet knife.

3 To make the salmon sushi, make a simple flat omelette by beating together the eggs, salt and sugar. Heat a large non-stick pan, pour in the egg mixture, stir briefly and leave to set. Transfer to a clean dishtowel and cool.

4 Place the nori on to a bamboo mat, cover with the omelette, and trim to size. Spread a layer of rice over the omelette, then lay strips of salmon across the width. Season the salmon with the thinned wasabi, then place a strip of cucumber next to the salmon. Fold the bamboo mat in half. Cut into neat rounds with a wet knife.

GREEN BEANS, RICE AND BEEF

SERVES 4

INGREDIENTS
    25g/1oz/2 tbsp butter or margarine
    1 large onion, chopped
    450g/1lb stewing beef, cubed
    2 garlic cloves, crushed
    5ml/1 tsp ground cinnamon
    5ml/1 tsp ground cumin
    5ml/1 tsp ground turmeric
    450g/1lb tomatoes, chopped
    30ml/2 tbsp tomato purée (paste)
    350ml/12fl oz/1$^{1}/_{2}$ cups water
    350g/12oz/2$^{1}/_{2}$ cups green beans,
        trimmed and halved
    salt and ground black pepper

For the rice
    275g/10oz/scant 1$^{1}/_{2}$ cups hasmati
        rice, soaked in salted water for
        2 hours
    1.75 litres/3 pints/7$^{1}/_{2}$ cups water
    45ml/3 tbsp melted butter
    2–3 saffron threads, soaked in
        15ml/1 tbsp boiling water
    pinch of salt

1 Melt the butter or margarine in a large pan or flameproof casserole and cook the onion until golden. Add the beef and cook until evenly browned, then add the garlic, spices, tomatoes, tomato purée and water. Season with salt and pepper. Bring to the boil, then simmer over a low heat for about 30 minutes.

2 Add the green beans and continue cooking for a further 15 minutes, until the meat is tender and most of the meat juices have evaporated.

3 Meanwhile, prepare the rice. Drain, then boil it in salted water for about 5 minutes. Reduce the heat and simmer very gently for 10 minutes or until it is half cooked. Drain, and rinse the rice in warm water. Wash and dry the pan.

4 Heat 15ml/1 tbsp of the melted butter in the pan and stir in about a third of the rice. Spoon half of the meat mixture over the rice, add a layer of rice, then the remaining meat and finish with another layer of rice.

5 Pour the remaining melted butter over the rice and cover the pan with a clean dishtowel. Cover with the lid and then steam the rice for 30–45 minutes over a low heat.

6 Take 45ml/3 tbsp of cooked rice from the pan and mix with the saffron water. Serve the cooked rice and beef on a large dish and sprinkle the saffron rice on top.

SWEET AND SOUR RICE

ZERESHK POLO *IS FLAVOURED WITH FRUIT AND SPICES AND IS COMMONLY SERVED WITH CHICKEN DISHES.*

SERVES 4

INGREDIENTS
  50g/2oz/¼ cup zereshk
  45ml/3 tbsp melted butter
  50g/2oz/⅓ cup raisins
  30ml/2 tbsp sugar
  5ml/1 tsp ground cinnamon
  5ml/1 tsp ground cumin
  350g/12oz/1¾ cups basmati rice,
    soaked in salted water for 2 hours
  2–3 saffron threads, soaked in 15ml/
    1 tbsp boiling water
  salt

1 Thoroughly wash the zereshk in cold water at least 4–5 times to rinse off any traces of grit.

2 Heat 15ml/1 tbsp of the butter in a small frying pan and stir-fry the raisins for 1–2 minutes.

3 Add the zereshk, fry for a few seconds and then add the sugar, and half of the cinnamon and cumin. Cook briefly and then set aside.

4 Drain the rice and then boil in salted water for 5 minutes, reduce the heat and simmer for 10 minutes, until half cooked.

5 Drain and rinse in lukewarm water and wash and dry the pan. Heat half of the remaining butter in the pan, add 15ml/ 1 tbsp water and stir in half of the rice.

6 Sprinkle with half of the raisin and zereshk mixture and top with all but 45ml/3 tbsp of the rice. Sprinkle over the remaining raisin mixture.

7 Blend the reserved rice with the remaining cinnamon and cumin and sprinkle over the top of the rice mixture. Drizzle the remaining butter over and then cover the pan with a clean dishtowel and secure with a tightly fitting lid, lifting the corners of the cloth back over the lid. Steam the rice over a very low heat for about 30–40 minutes.

8 Just before serving, mix 45ml/3 tbsp of the rice with the saffron water. Spoon the rice on to a large flat serving dish and sprinkle the saffron rice over the top to garnish.

COOK'S TIP
Zereshk are very small dried berries that are delicious mixed with rice. They are available from most Persian and Middle Eastern food stores.

BAMIE GORENG

*THIS FRIED NOODLE DISH IS WONDERFULLY ACCOMMODATING. TO THE BASIC RECIPE YOU CAN ADD OTHER
VEGETABLES, SUCH AS MUSHROOMS, TINY PIECES OF CHAYOTE, BROCCOLI, LEEKS OR BEANSPROUTS, IF YOU
PREFER. AS WITH FRIED RICE, YOU CAN USE WHATEVER YOU HAVE TO HAND, BEARING IN MIND THE NEED TO
ACHIEVE A BALANCE OF COLOURS, FLAVOURS AND TEXTURES.*

SERVES 6–8

INGREDIENTS
450g/1lb dried egg noodles
1 boneless, skinless chicken breast portion
115g/4oz pork fillet (tenderloin)
115g/4oz calf's liver (optional)
2 eggs, beaten
90ml/6 tbsp oil
25g/1oz/2 tbsp butter or margarine
2 garlic cloves, crushed
115g/4oz/1 cup cooked, peeled
  prawns (shrimp)
115g/4oz spinach or Chinese leaves
  (Chinese cabbage)
2 celery sticks, finely sliced
4 spring onions (scallions), shredded
about 60ml/4 tbsp chicken stock
dark soy sauce and light soy sauce
salt and ground black pepper
deep-fried onions and celery leaves,
  to garnish

1 Cook the noodles in salted, boiling water for 3–4 minutes. Drain, rinse with cold water and drain again. Set aside until required.

2 Finely slice the chicken, pork fillet and calf's liver, if using.

3 Season the eggs. Heat 5ml/1 tsp oil with the butter or margarine in a small pan until melted and then stir in the eggs and keep stirring until scrambled. Set aside.

4 Heat the remaining oil in a wok and cook the garlic with the chicken, pork and liver for 2–3 minutes, until they have changed colour. Add the prawns, spinach or Chinese leaves, celery and spring onions, tossing well.

5 Add the cooked and drained noodles and toss well again so that all the ingredients are well mixed. Add enough stock just to moisten and dark and light soy sauce to taste. Finally, stir in the scrambled eggs.

6 Serve, garnished with deep-fried onions and celery leaves.

RICE WITH DILL AND SPICY BEANS

THIS SPICED RICE DISH IS A FAVOURITE IN IRAN, WHERE IT IS KNOWN AS BAGHALI POLO.

SERVES 4

INGREDIENTS

275g/10oz/scant 1½ cups basmati
   rice, soaked in salted water for
   3 hours
45ml/3 tbsp melted butter
175g/6oz/1½ cups broad (fava) beans,
   fresh or frozen
90ml/6 tbsp finely chopped fresh dill
5ml/1 tsp ground cinnamon
5ml/1 tsp ground cumin
2–3 saffron threads, soaked in 15ml/
   1 tbsp boiling water
salt

1 Drain the rice and then boil it in fresh salted water for 5 minutes. Reduce the heat and simmer very gently for 10 minutes, until half cooked. Drain and rinse in warm water.

2 Put 15ml/1 tbsp of the butter in a non-stick pan and add enough rice to cover the base. Add a quarter of the beans and a little dill.

3 Add another layer of rice, then a layer of beans and dill and continue layering until all the beans and dill are used up, finishing with a layer of rice. Cook over a low heat for 10 minutes.

4 Pour the remaining melted butter over the rice. Sprinkle with the cinnamon and cumin. Cover the pan with a clean dishtowel and secure with a tight-fitting lid, lifting the corners of the cloth back over the lid. Steam over a low heat for 30–45 minutes.

5 Mix 45ml/3 tbsp of the rice with the saffron water. Spoon the remaining rice on to a large serving plate and sprinkle on the saffron-flavoured rice to decorate. Serve with either a lamb or chicken dish.

COOK'S TIP
Saffron may seem expensive, however you only need a little to add flavour and colour to a variety of savoury and sweet dishes. And, as long as it is kept dry and dark, it never goes off.

MEXICAN-STYLE RICE

SERVES 6

INGREDIENTS

350g/12oz/1³/₄ cups long grain white rice
1 onion, chopped
2 garlic cloves, chopped
450g/1lb tomatoes, peeled, seeded and
    coarsely chopped
60ml/4 tbsp corn or groundnut
    (peanut) oil
900ml/1¹/₂ pints/3³/₄ cups chicken stock
4–6 small red chillies
175g/6oz/1 cup cooked green peas
salt and ground black pepper
fresh coriander (cilantro) sprigs,
    to garnish

1 Soak the rice in a bowl of hot water for 15 minutes. Drain, rinse well under cold running water, drain again and set aside.

2 Combine the onion, garlic and tomatoes in a food processor and process to a purée.

3 Heat the oil in a large frying pan. Add the drained rice and sauté until it is golden brown. Using a slotted spoon, transfer the rice to a pan.

4 Reheat the oil remaining in the pan and cook the tomato purée for 2–3 minutes. Tip it into the rice pan, pour in the stock and season. Bring to the boil, reduce the heat to the lowest setting, cover the pan and cook for 15–20 minutes, until almost all the liquid is absorbed. Slice the chillies from tip to stem into four or five sections. Place in a bowl of iced water until they curl back to form flowers, then drain.

5 Stir the peas into the rice mixture and cook, uncovered, until the liquid has been absorbed and the rice is tender. Stir the mixture occasionally.

6 Transfer the rice to a serving dish and garnish with the drained chilli flowers and sprigs of coriander. Warn the diners that these elaborate chilli "flowers" are hot and should be approached with caution.

TOSSED NOODLES WITH SEAFOOD

SERVES 4–6

INGREDIENTS

350g/12oz thick egg noodles
60ml/4 tbsp vegetable oil
3 slices fresh root ginger, grated
2 garlic cloves, finely chopped
225g/8oz mussels or clams
225g/8oz raw prawns (shrimp), peeled
225g/8oz squid, cut into rings
115g/4oz Asian fried fish cake, sliced
1 red (bell) pepper, seeded and cut
    into rings
50g/2oz sugar snap peas, trimmed
30ml/2 tbsp soy sauce
2.5ml/½ tsp sugar
120ml/4fl oz/½ cup stock or water
15ml/1 tbsp cornflour (cornstarch)
5–10ml/1–2 tsp sesame oil
salt and ground black pepper
2 spring onions (scallions), chopped,
    and 2 red chillies, seeded and
    chopped, to garnish

1 Cook the noodles in a large pan of boiling water until just tender. Drain, rinse under cold water and drain well.

2 Heat the oil in a wok or large frying pan. Fry the ginger and garlic for 30 seconds. Add the mussels or clams, prawns and squid and stir-fry for about 4–5 minutes, until the seafood changes colour. Add the fish cake slices, red pepper rings and sugar snap peas and stir well.

3 In a bowl, mix the soy sauce, sugar, stock or water and cornflour. Stir into the seafood and bring to the boil. Add the noodles and cook until heated through.

4 Add the sesame oil to the wok or pan and season with salt and pepper to taste. Serve immediately, garnished with the spring onions and red chillies.

NOODLES WITH SPICY MEAT SAUCE

SERVES 4–6

INGREDIENTS

30ml/2 tbsp vegetable oil
2 dried red chillies, chopped
5ml/1 tsp grated fresh root ginger
2 garlic cloves, finely chopped
15ml/1 tbsp chilli bean paste
450g/1lb minced (ground) pork or beef
450g/1lb broad flat egg noodles
15ml/1 tbsp sesame oil
2 spring onions (scallions), chopped,
    to garnish

For the sauce
1.25ml/¼ tsp salt
5ml/1 tsp sugar
15ml/1 tbsp soy sauce
5ml/1 tsp mushroom ketchup
15ml/1 tbsp cornflour (cornstarch)
250ml/8fl oz/1 cup chicken stock
5ml/1 tsp Chinese rice wine or
    dry sherry

1 Heat the vegetable oil in a large pan. Add the dried chillies, ginger and garlic. Cook until the garlic starts to colour, then gradually stir in the chilli bean paste.

2 Add the minced pork or beef, breaking it up with a spatula or wooden spoon. Cook over a high heat until the minced meat changes colour and any liquid has been evaporated.

3 Mix all the sauce ingredients in a jug (pitcher). Make a well in the centre of the pork mixture. Pour in the sauce mixture and stir together. Simmer for about 10–15 minutes, until tender.

4 Meanwhile, cook the noodles in a large pan of boiling water for 5–7 minutes, until just tender. Drain well and toss with the sesame oil. Serve, topped with the meat sauce and garnished with the spring onions.

TOMATO NOODLES WITH FRIED EGG

SERVES 4

INGREDIENTS

350g/12oz medium-thick
   dried noodles
60ml/4 tbsp vegetable oil
2 garlic cloves, very
   finely chopped
4 shallots, chopped
2.5ml/¹/₂ tsp chilli powder
5ml/1 tsp paprika
2 carrots, finely diced
115g/4oz button (white)
   mushrooms, quartered
50g/2oz/¹/₂ cup peas
15ml/1 tbsp tomato ketchup
10ml/2 tsp tomato purée (paste)
salt and ground black pepper
butter, for frying
4 eggs

1 Cook the noodles in a pan of boiling water until just tender. Drain, rinse under cold running water and drain well.

2 Heat the oil in a wok or large frying pan. Add the garlic, shallots, chilli powder and paprika. Stir-fry for about 1 minute, then add the carrots, mushrooms and peas. Continue to stir-fry until the vegetables are cooked.

3 Stir the tomato ketchup and purée into the vegetable mixture. Add the noodles and cook over a medium heat until the noodles are heated through and have taken on the reddish tinge of the paprika and tomato.

4 Meanwhile, melt the butter in a frying pan and fry the eggs. Season the noodle mixture, divide it among four serving plates and top each portion with a fried egg.

CURRY FRIED NOODLES

ON ITS OWN TOFU, HAS A FAIRLY BLAND FLAVOUR, BUT IT TAKES ON THE FLAVOURS OF OTHER INGREDIENTS, SUCH AS THE CURRY SPICES USED HERE, QUITE WONDERFULLY.

SERVES 4

INGREDIENTS

60ml/4 tbsp vegetable oil
30–45ml/2–3 tbsp curry paste
225g/8oz smoked tofu, cut into
   2.5cm/1in cubes
225g/8oz/1¹/₂ cups green beans, cut
   into 2.5cm/1in lengths
1 red (bell) pepper, seeded and cut
   into fine strips
350g/12oz rice vermicelli, soaked in
   warm water until soft
15ml/1 tbsp soy sauce
salt and ground black pepper
2 spring onions (scallions), finely
   sliced, 2 red chillies, seeded and
   chopped, and 1 lime, cut into
   wedges, to garnish

1 Heat half the oil in a wok or large frying pan. Add the curry paste and stir-fry for a few minutes, then add the tofu and continue to stir-fry until golden brown. Using a slotted spoon remove the cubes from the pan and set aside until required.

2 Add the remaining oil to the wok or pan. When hot, add the green beans and red pepper. Stir-fry until the vegetables are cooked. You may need to moisten them with a little water.

3 Drain the noodles and add them to the wok or frying pan. Continue to stir-fry until the noodles are heated through, then return the curried tofu to the wok. Season with soy sauce, salt and pepper.

4 Transfer the mixture to a serving dish. Sprinkle with the spring onions and chillies and serve the lime wedges on the side.

PENNE WITH CHILLI AND BROCCOLI

SERVES 4

INGREDIENTS

450g/1lb/3 cups penne
450g/1lb small broccoli florets
30ml/2 tbsp stock
1 garlic clove, crushed
1 small red chilli, sliced, or 2.5ml/
   ½ tsp chilli sauce
60ml/4 tbsp natural (plain) yogurt
30ml/2 tbsp toasted pine nuts
   or cashews
salt and ground black pepper

VARIATION
Green chillies can be used instead of
red chillies and toasted almonds make
a good substitute for pine nuts.

1 Add the pasta to a large pan of lightly
salted, boiling water and return to the
boil. Place the broccoli in a steamer
basket over the top. Cover and cook for
8–10 minutes, until both are just tender,
then drain.

2 Heat the stock and add the crushed
garlic and chilli or chilli sauce. Stir over
a low heat for 2–3 minutes.

3 Stir in the broccoli, pasta and yogurt.
Adjust the seasoning, sprinkle with nuts
and serve hot.

CRISPY FRIED RICE VERMICELLI – MEE KROB

*MEE KROB IS USUALLY SERVED AT THAI CELEBRATION MEALS. IT IS A CRISP TANGLE OF FRIED RICE
VERMICELLI, TOSSED IN A PIQUANT GARLIC, SWEET AND SOUR SAUCE.*

SERVES 4–6

INGREDIENTS
oil, for frying
175g/6oz rice vermicelli
15ml/1 tbsp chopped garlic
4–6 dried chillies, seeded and
  chopped
30ml/2 tbsp chopped shallot
15ml/1 tbsp dried shrimp, rinsed
115g/4oz/1 cup minced (ground) pork
115g/4oz/1 cup raw prawns (shrimp),
  peeled and chopped
30ml/2 tbsp brown bean sauce
30ml/2 tbsp rice wine vinegar
45ml/3 tbsp fish sauce
75g/3 tbsp palm sugar
30ml/2 tbsp tamarind or lime juice
115g/4oz/2 cups beansprouts

For the garnish
2 spring onions (scallions), shredded
30ml/2 tbsp fresh coriander (cilantro)
  leaves
2 heads pickled garlic (optional)
2-egg omelette, rolled and sliced
2 red chillies, chopped

3 Add the minced pork and stir-fry until
it is no longer pink, about 3–4 minutes.
Add the prawns and stir-fry for a further
2 minutes. Remove the mixture from the
wok and set aside.

4 To the same wok, add the brown bean
sauce, vinegar, fish sauce and palm
sugar. Bring to a gentle boil, stir to
dissolve the sugar and cook until thick
and syrupy.

6 Reduce the heat. Add the pork and
prawn mixture and the beansprouts to the
sauce, stir to mix.

7 Add the rice noodles and toss gently to
coat them with the sauce without breaking
the noodles too much. Transfer the
noodles to a platter. Garnish with spring
onions, coriander leaves, pickled garlic,
omelette strips and red chillies.

1 Heat the oil in a wok. Break the rice
vermicelli apart into small handfuls about
7.5cm/3in long. Deep-fry in the hot oil
until they puff up. Remove and drain on
kitchen paper.

2 Leave 30ml/2 tbsp of the hot oil in the
wok, add the garlic, chillies, shallots and
shrimp. Fry until fragrant.

5 Add the tamarind or lime juice and
adjust the seasoning. It should be sweet,
sour and salty.

VEGETARIAN FRIED NOODLES

TOFU ADDS FOOD VALUE TO THIS DELICIOUSLY SATISFYING HOT AND SPICY NOODLE DISH THAT WILL BECOME A FIRM FAVOURITE WITH YOUNG AND OLD ALIKE.

SERVES 4

INGREDIENTS

2 eggs
5ml/1 tsp chilli powder
5ml/1 tsp ground turmeric
60ml/4 tbsp vegetable oil
1 large onion, finely sliced
2 red chillies, seeded and
  finely sliced
15ml/1 tbsp soy sauce
2 large cooked potatoes, cut into
  small cubes
6 pieces fried tofu, sliced
225g/8oz/4 cups beansprouts
115g/4oz/³/4 cup green
  beans, blanched
350g/12oz fresh thick egg noodles
salt and ground black pepper
sliced spring onions (scallions),
  to garnish

1 Beat the eggs lightly, then strain them into a bowl. Heat a lightly greased omelette pan. Pour in half of the egg to cover the base of the pan thinly. When the egg is just set, turn the omelette over and cook the other side briefly. Slide on to a plate, blot with kitchen paper, roll up and cut into narrow strips. Make a second omelette in the same way and slice. Set the omelette strips aside for the garnish.

COOK'S TIP
When making this dish for non-vegetarians, add a piece of compressed shrimp paste. A small chunk about the size of a stock cube, mashed with the chilli paste, will add a deliciously rich, aromatic flavour.

2 In a cup, mix together the chilli powder and turmeric. Form a paste by stirring in a little water.

3 Heat the oil in a wok or large frying pan. Cook the onion until soft, Reduce the heat and add the chilli paste, sliced chillies and soy sauce. Stir-fry for 2–3 minutes.

4 Add the potatoes and stir-fry for about 2 minutes, mixing well with the chillies. Add the tofu, then the beansprouts, green beans and noodles.

5 Gently stir-fry until the noodles are evenly coated and heated through. Take care not to break up the potatoes or the tofu. Season with salt and pepper. Serve hot, garnished with the reserved omelette strips and spring onion slices.

THAI FRIED NOODLES

PHAT THAI *HAS A FASCINATING FLAVOUR AND TEXTURE. IT IS MADE WITH RICE NOODLES AND IS CONSIDERED ONE OF THE NATIONAL DISHES OF THAILAND.*

SERVES 4–6

INGREDIENTS
    350g/12oz rice noodles
    45ml/3 tbsp vegetable oil
    15ml/1 tbsp chopped garlic
    16 uncooked king prawns (jumbo
      shrimp), peeled, tails left intact
      and deveined
    2 eggs, lightly beaten
    15ml/1 tbsp dried shrimp, rinsed
    30ml/2 tbsp pickled white radish
    50g/2oz fried tofu, cut into small
      slivers
    2.5ml/½ tsp dried chilli flakes
    115g/4oz garlic chives, cut into
      5cm/2in lengths
    225g/8oz/4 cups beansprouts
    50g/2oz/½ cup roasted peanuts,
      coarsely ground
    5ml/1 tsp sugar
    15ml/1 tbsp dark soy sauce
    30ml/2 tbsp fish sauce
    30ml/2 tbsp tamarind juice
    30ml/2 tbsp coriander (cilantro)
      leaves, to garnish
    1 kaffir lime, to garnish

1 Soak the noodles in warm water for 20–30 minutes, then drain.

2 Heat 15ml/1 tbsp of the oil in a wok or large frying pan. Add the garlic and stir-fry until golden. Stir in the prawns and cook for 1–2 minutes until pink, tossing occasionally. Remove and set aside.

3 Heat another 15ml/1 tbsp of oil in the wok. Add the eggs and tilt the wok to spread them into a thin sheet. Stir to scramble and break the egg into small pieces. Remove from the wok and set aside with the prawns.

4 Heat the remaining oil in the same wok. Add the dried shrimp, pickled radish, tofu and dried chillies. Stir briefly. Add the soaked noodles and stir-fry for 5 minutes.

5 Add the garlic chives, half the beansprouts and half the peanuts. Season with the sugar, soy sauce, fish sauce and tamarind juice. Mix well and cook until the noodles are heated through.

6 Return the prawn and egg mixture to the wok and mix with the noodles. Serve garnished with the rest of the beansprouts, peanuts, coriander leaves and lime wedges.

SPICY SICHUAN NOODLES

SERVES 4

INGREDIENTS
  350g/12oz thick noodles
  175g/6oz cooked chicken,
    shredded
  50g/2oz/½ cup roasted cashew nuts

For the dressing
  4 spring onions (scallions), chopped
  30ml/2 tbsp chopped coriander
    (cilantro)
  2 garlic cloves, chopped
  30ml/2 tbsp smooth peanut butter
  30ml/2 tbsp sweet chilli sauce
  15ml/1 tbsp soy sauce
  15ml/1 tbsp sherry vinegar
  15ml/1 tbsp sesame oil
  30ml/2 tbsp olive oil
  30ml/2 tbsp chicken stock
    or water
  10 toasted Sichuan peppercorns,
    ground

1 Cook the noodles in a pan of boiling water until just tender, following the directions on the packet. Drain, rinse under cold running water and drain well.

2 While the noodles are cooking combine all the ingredients for the dressing in a large bowl and whisk together well.

3 Add the noodles, shredded chicken and cashew nuts to the dressing, toss gently to coat and adjust the seasoning to taste. Serve immediately.

COOK'S TIP   .
You could substitute cooked turkey or pork for the chicken for a change.

SESAME NOODLES WITH SPRING ONIONS

THIS SIMPLE BUT VERY TASTY WARM SALAD CAN BE PREPARED AND COOKED IN JUST A FEW MINUTES.

SERVES 4

INGREDIENTS
  2 garlic cloves, coarsely chopped
  30ml/2 tbsp Chinese sesame paste
  15ml/1 tbsp dark sesame oil
  30ml/2 tbsp soy sauce
  30ml/2 tbsp rice wine
  15ml/1 tbsp honey
  pinch of five-spice powder
  350g/12oz soba or
    buckwheat noodles
  4 spring onions (scallions), finely
    sliced diagonally
  50g/2oz/1 cup beansprouts
  7.5cm/3in piece of cucumber, cut
    into batons
  toasted sesame seeds
  salt and ground black pepper

1 Process the garlic, sesame paste, oil, soy sauce, rice wine, honey and five-spice powder with a pinch each of salt and pepper in a blender or food processor until smooth.

2 Cook the noodles in a pan of boiling water until just tender, following the directions on the packet. Drain the noodles immediately and tip them into a bowl.

3 Toss the hot noodles with the dressing and the spring onions. Top with the beansprouts, cucumber and sesame seeds and serve.

COOK'S TIP
If you can't find Chinese sesame paste, then use either tahini paste or smooth peanut butter instead.

Plain meat, poultry or fish are delicious when spiced up

with a red-hot salsa, chutney, relish or pickle. The

selection varies from Coconut Chilli Relish, which is

pleasantly hot, to scorchingly hot Double Chilli Salsa.

Tomato and Onion Salad with red chilli is surprisingly

refreshing, and Pickled Cucumbers are good with all

kinds of cold meats or cheese.

Searing-hot Side Dishes, Salsas and Relishes

TOMATO AND ONION SALAD

ALSO KNOWN AS ATJAR KETIMUN, THIS IS A REFRESHING SALAD THAT CAN BE MADE AHEAD.. IT IMPROVES IF WELL CHILLED BEFORE SERVING. USE ONLY FIRM, SLIGHTLY UNDER-RIPE TOMATOES SO THAT THE FLESH DOES NOT COLLAPSE WHEN CUT INTO DICE.

SERVES 6

INGREDIENTS

    1 cucumber
    45ml/3 tbsp good-quality rice or white
        wine vinegar
    10ml/2 tsp sugar
    1 tomato, peeled, seeded and diced
    1 small onion, finely sliced
    1 fresh red chilli, seeded and chopped
    salt

1 Trim the ends from the cucumber. Peel it lengthways but leave some of the skin on to make the salad more attractive. Cut in thin slices and lay them out on a large plate. Sprinkle with a little salt and leave for about 15 minutes. Rinse well and dry.

2 Mix the vinegar, sugar and a pinch of salt together. Arrange all the vegetables in a bowl and pour over the vinegar, sugar and salt mixture. Cover the salad and chill before serving.

COCONUT AND PEANUT RELISH

THE AROMA OF TOASTED COCONUT IS WONDERFUL AND IMMEDIATELY WILL HAVE YOU DREAMING OF WARMER CLIMES! SERUDENG IS SERVED AS AN ACCOMPANIMENT TO MANY INDONESIAN DISHES; ANY LEFTOVERS CAN BE STORED IN AN AIRTIGHT BOX.

SERVES 6–8

INGREDIENTS

    115g/4oz/1¹/3 cups grated fresh
        coconut, or desiccated (dry
        unsweetened
        shredded) coconut
    175g/6oz salted peanuts
    5mm/¹/4 in cube shrimp paste
    1 small onion, quartered
    2–3 garlic cloves, crushed
    45ml/3 tbsp oil
    2.5ml/¹/2 tsp tamarind pulp, soaked in
        30ml/2 tbsp warm water
    5ml/1 tsp coriander seeds, dry-fried
        and ground
    2.5ml/¹/2 tsp cumin seeds, dry-fried
        and ground
    5ml/1 tsp dark brown sugar

1 Dry-fry the coconut in a wok or large frying pan over a medium heat, turning constantly, until crisp and a rich, golden colour. Leave to cool and add half to the peanuts. Toss together to mix.

2 Grind the shrimp paste, with the onion and garlic, to a paste in a food processor or with a mortar and pestle. Stir-fry in hot oil, without browning. Strain the tamarind and reserve the juice. Add the coriander, cumin, tamarind juice and brown sugar to the fried paste. Stir constantly and cook for 2–3 minutes.

3 Stir in the remaining toasted coconut and leave to cool. When quite cold, mix with the peanut and coconut mixture.

FIERY CITRUS SALSA

THIS VERY UNUSUAL SALSA MAKES A FANTASTIC MARINADE FOR ALL KINDS OF SHELLFISH AND IT IS ALSO DELICIOUS WHEN DRIZZLED OVER MEAT COOKED ON THE BARBECUE.

SERVES 4

INGREDIENTS
    1 orange
    1 green apple
    2 fresh red chillies, halved and seeded
    1 garlic clove
    8 fresh mint leaves
    juice of 1 lemon
    salt and ground black pepper

1 Slice the base off the orange so it stands firmly on a chopping board. Using a sharp knife, remove the peel by slicing from the top to the bottom of the orange.

2 Hold the orange in one hand over a bowl. Slice towards the middle of the fruit, to one side of a segment, and then gently twist the knife to ease the segment away from the membrane and out of the orange. Repeat to remove all the segments. Squeeze any juice from the remaining membrane.

3 Peel the apple, slice it into wedges and remove the core.

4 Place the chillies in a blender or food processor with the orange segments and juice, apple wedges, garlic and mint.

5 Process until smooth, then, with the motor running, pour in the lemon juice.

6 Season, pour into a bowl or small jug (pitcher) and serve immediately.

VARIATION
If you're feeling really fiery, don't seed the chillies! They will make the salsa particularly hot and fierce.

SALSA VERDE

THERE ARE MANY VERSIONS OF THIS CLASSIC GREEN SALSA. SERVE THIS ONE WITH CREAMY MASHED POTATOES OR DRIZZLED OVER THE TOP OF CHARGRILLED SQUID.

SERVES 4

INGREDIENTS

2–4 green chillies
8 spring onions (scallions)
2 garlic cloves
50g/2oz/¹/₂ cup salted capers
fresh tarragon sprig
1 bunch of fresh parsley
grated rind and juice of 1 lime
juice of 1 lemon
90ml/6 tbsp olive oil
about 15ml/1 tbsp green Tabasco
  sauce, or to taste
ground black pepper

1 Halve the green chillies and remove their seeds. Trim the spring onions and halve the garlic, then place in a food processor or blender. Pulse the power briefly until the ingredients are coarsely chopped.

2 Use your fingertips to rub the excess salt off the capers but do not rinse them. Add the capers, tarragon and parsley to the food processor or blender and pulse again until they are fairly finely chopped.

VARIATION
If you can find only capers pickled in vine-gar, they can be used for this salsa but they must be rinsed well in cold water first.

3 Transfer the mixture to a small bowl. Stir in the lime rind and juice, lemon juice and olive oil. Stir the mixture lightly so the citrus juice and oil do not emulsify.

4 Add green Tabasco and ground black pepper to taste. Chill the salsa until ready to serve, but do not prepare more than 8 hours in advance.

BERRY SALSA

INGREDIENTS
1 fresh jalapeño chilli
$^1/_2$ red onion, chopped
2 spring onions (scallions), chopped
1 tomato, finely diced
1 small yellow (bell) pepper, seeded
  and chopped
60ml/4 tbsp chopped fresh
  coriander (cilantro)
1.5ml/$^1/_4$ tsp salt
15ml/1 tbsp raspberry vinegar
15ml/1 tbsp fresh orange juice
5ml/1 tsp honey
15ml/1 tbsp olive oil
150g/5oz/1 cup strawberries, hulled
115g/4oz/1 cup blueberries or blackberries
175g/6oz/1 cup raspberries

1 Wearing rubber gloves, finely chop the jalapeño chilli. Discard the seeds and membrane if you prefer a less hot flavour. Place the chilli in a bowl.

2 Add the red onion, spring onions, tomato, pepper and coriander, and stir well to blend.

3 In a small mixing bowl or jug (pitcher), whisk together the salt, raspberry vinegar, orange juice, honey and olive oil. Pour this over the jalapeño mixture and stir well to combine.

4 Coarsely chop the strawberries. Add them to the jalapeño mixture with the blueberries or blackberries and the raspberries. Stir to blend together. Stand at room temperature for about 3 hours.

5 Serve the salsa at room temperature, with grilled (broiled) fish or poultry.

MIXED VEGETABLE PICKLE

IF YOU CAN OBTAIN FRESH TURMERIC, IT MAKES SUCH A DIFFERENCE TO THE COLOUR AND APPEARANCE OF ACAR CAMPUR. YOU CAN USE ALMOST ANY VEGETABLE, BEARING IN MIND THAT YOU NEED A BALANCE OF TEXTURES, FLAVOURS AND COLOURS.

MAKES 2–3 X 300G/11OZ JARS

INGREDIENTS
1 fresh red chilli, seeded and sliced
1 onion, quartered
2 garlic cloves, crushed
1cm/$\frac{1}{2}$ in cube shrimp paste
4 macadamia nuts or 8 almonds
2.5cm/1in fresh turmeric, peeled and
   sliced, or 5ml/1 tsp ground turmeric
50ml/2fl oz/$\frac{1}{4}$ cup sunflower oil
475ml/16fl oz/2 cups white vinegar
250ml/8fl oz/1 cup water
25–50g/1–2oz sugar
3 carrots
225g/8oz/1$\frac{1}{2}$ cups green beans
1 small cauliflower
1 cucumber
225g/8oz white cabbage
115g/4oz/1 cup dry-roasted peanuts,
   coarsely crushed
salt

1 Place the chilli, onion, garlic, shrimp paste, nuts and turmeric in a food processor and blend to a paste, or pound in a mortar with a pestle.

2 Heat the oil and stir-fry the paste to release the aroma. Add the vinegar, water, sugar and salt. Bring to the boil. Simmer for 10 minutes.

COOK'S TIP
This pickle is even better if you make it a few days ahead.

3 Cut the carrots into flower shapes. Cut the green beans into short, neat lengths. Separate the cauliflower into neat, bitesize florets. Peel and seed the cucumber and cut the flesh in neat, bitesize pieces. Cut the cabbage in neat, bitesize pieces.

4 Blanch each vegetable separately, in a large pan of boiling water, for 1 minute. Transfer to a colander and rinse with cold water, to halt the cooking. Drain well.

5 Add the vegetables to the sauce. Gradually bring to the boil and cook for 5–10 minutes. Do not overcook – the vegetables should still be quite crunchy.

6 Add the peanuts and cool. Spoon into clean jars with lids.

APRICOT CHUTNEY

CHUTNEYS CAN ADD ZEST TO MOST MEALS, AND IN PAKISTAN YOU WILL USUALLY FIND A SELECTION OF DIFFERENT KINDS SERVED IN TINY BOWLS FOR PEOPLE TO CHOOSE FROM. DRIED APRICOTS ARE READILY AVAILABLE FROM SUPERMARKETS OR HEALTH FOOD STORES.

MAKES ABOUT 450G/1LB

INGREDIENTS
450g/1lb/3 cups dried apricots,
  finely chopped
5ml/1 tsp garam masala
275g/10oz/1¼ cups soft light
  brown sugar
450ml/16fl oz/2 cups malt vinegar
5ml/1 tsp ginger pulp
5ml/1 tsp salt
75g/3oz/½ cup sultanas
  (golden raisins)
450ml/16fl oz/2 cups water

1 Put all of the ingredients into a medium pan and mix them together thoroughly.

2 Bring the mixture to the boil, then turn down the heat and simmer for 30–35 minutes, stirring occasionally as it cooks.

3 When the chutney has thickened to a fairly stiff consistency, transfer it to two or three clean jam jars and leave to cool thoroughly. This chutney should be covered tightly with a lid and stored in the refrigerator.

VARIATION
For a change, you could try dried peaches instead of apricots. If you like, you can add heat with green chillies.

TASTY TOASTS

THESE CRUNCHY TOASTS HAVE A WONDERFUL SPICY FLAVOUR. THEY MAKE AN IDEAL SNACK OR PART OF A WEEKEND BRUNCH. THEY ARE ESPECIALLY DELICIOUS WHEN SERVED WITH FRESHLY GRILLED TOMATOES AND BAKED BEANS.

SERVES 4

INGREDIENTS
4 eggs
300ml/½ pint/1¼ cups milk
2 fresh green chillies, finely chopped
30ml/2 tbsp chopped fresh coriander
  (cilantro)
75g/3oz/¾ cup grated Cheddar or
  mozzarella cheese
2.5ml/½ tsp salt
1.5ml/¼ tsp ground black pepper
4 slices bread
corn oil, for frying

1 Break the eggs into a medium bowl and whisk together. Slowly add the milk and whisk again. Add the green chillies, fresh coriander, grated cheese and salt and pepper to taste.

2 Cut the bread slices in half diagonally, and soak them, one at a time, in the egg mixture.

3 Heat the corn oil in a medium frying pan and fry the soaked bread slices over a medium heat, turning them once or twice, until they are golden brown.

4 Drain off any excess oil as you remove the toasts from the pan and serve them immediately.

DOUBLE CHILLI SALSA

ONLY THE VERY BRAVE SHOULD SAMPLE THIS SCORCHINGLY HOT SALSA! SPREAD IT SPARINGLY ON TO COOKED MEATS AND BURGERS.

SERVES 4–6

INGREDIENTS

    6 habanero chillies or Scotch bonnets
    2 ripe tomatoes
    4 green jalapeño chillies
    30ml/2 tbsp chopped fresh parsley
    30ml/2 tbsp olive oil
    15ml/1 tbsp balsamic or sherry vinegar
    salt

1 Skewer an habanero chilli on a metal fork and hold it in a gas flame for about 2–3 minutes, turning until the skin blackens and blisters. Repeat with all the chillies, then set aside.

3 Use a clean dishtowel to rub the skins off the chillies.

COOK'S TIP
Habanero chillies, or Scotch bonnets, are among the hottest fresh chillies available. You may prefer to tone down the heat of this salsa by using a milder variety.

2 Skewer and blister the tomatoes in the flame for 1–2 minutes, until the skin splits and wrinkles. Slip off the skins, halve the tomatoes, then use a teaspoon to scoop out and discard the seeds. Chop the flesh very finely.

4 Try not to touch the chillies with your bare hands: use a fork to hold them and slice them open with a sharp knife. Scrape out and discard the seeds, then finely chop the flesh.

5 Halve the jalapeño chillies, then remove their seeds and slice finely widthways into tiny strips. Mix together both types of chilli, the tomatoes and the parsley.

6 Mix the olive oil, vinegar and a little salt, pour this over the salsa and cover the dish. The salsa will keep in the refrigerator for up to 3 days.

PIQUANT PINEAPPLE RELISH

THIS FRUITY SWEET AND SOUR RELISH IS REALLY EXCELLENT WHEN IT IS SERVED WITH GRILLED CHICKEN OR BACON SLICES.

SERVES 4

INGREDIENTS
    400g/14oz can crushed pineapple in
        natural juice
    30ml/2 tbsp light muscovado (brown)
        sugar
    30ml/2 tbsp wine vinegar
    1 garlic clove
    4 spring onions (scallions)
    2 red chillies
    10 fresh basil leaves
    salt and ground black pepper

1 Drain the crushed pineapple pieces thoroughly and reserve about 60ml/4 tbsp of the juice.

2 Place the juice in a small pan with the muscovado sugar and wine vinegar, then heat gently, stirring, until the sugar dissolves. Remove the pan from the heat and add salt and pepper to taste.

COOK'S TIP
This relish tastes extra special when made with fresh pineapple – substitute the juice of a freshly squeezed orange for the canned juice.

3 Finely chop the garlic and spring onions. Halve the chillies, remove the seeds and finely chop the flesh. Finely shred the basil.

4 Place the pineapple, garlic, spring onions and chillies in a bowl. Mix well and pour in the sauce. Leave to cool for 5 minutes, then stir in the basil.

PICKLED CUCUMBERS

OFTEN SERVED WITH SALT BEEF, THESE GHERKINS OR CUCUMBERS ARE SIMPLE TO PREPARE BUT TAKE A COUPLE OF DAYS FOR THE FLAVOUR TO DEVELOP.

SERVES 6–8

INGREDIENTS

    6 small pickling cucumbers
    75ml/5 tbsp white wine vinegar
    475ml/16fl oz/2 cups cold water
    15ml/1 tbsp salt
    10ml/2 tsp sugar
    10 black peppercorns
    1 garlic clove
    1 bunch fresh dill (optional)

1 You will need a large lidded jar or an oblong non-metallic container with a tightly fitting lid. Cut each cucumber lengthways into six spears.

2 Mix together the wine vinegar, water, salt and sugar. Crush a few of the peppercorns and leave the rest whole. Add them to the liquid. Cut the garlic clove in half.

3 Arrange the cucumber spears in the jar or container, pour over the pickling liquid and add the garlic. Put in a few sprigs of dill if using. Make sure they are completely submerged.

4 Leave the cucumbers, covered, in the refrigerator for at least two days. To serve, lift them out and discard the garlic, dill and peppercorns. Store any uneaten cucumbers in their pickling liquid in the refrigerator.

SPICY FRIED DUMPLINS

*SPICY FRIED DUMPLINS ARE VERY EASY TO MAKE. IN THE CARIBBEAN, THEY ARE OFTEN SERVED WITH
SALTFISH OR FRIED FISH, BUT THEY CAN BE EATEN QUITE SIMPLY WITH BUTTER AND JAM OR CHEESE.*

MAKES ABOUT 10

INGREDIENTS

450g/1lb/4 cups self-raising
(self-rising) flour
10ml/2 tsp sugar
2.5ml/$\frac{1}{2}$ tsp ground cinnamon
pinch of ground nutmeg
2.5ml/$\frac{1}{2}$ tsp salt
300ml/$\frac{1}{2}$ pint/1$\frac{1}{4}$ cups milk
oil, for frying

1 Sift the dry ingredients together into a
large bowl, add the milk and mix and
knead until smooth.

2 Divide the dough into ten balls,
kneading each ball with floured hands.
Press the balls gently to flatten into
7.5cm/3in rounds.

3 Heat a little oil in a non-stick frying pan
until moderately hot. Place half the
dumplins in the pan, reduce the heat to
low and cook for about 15 minutes until
they are golden brown, turning once.

4 Stand them on their sides for a few
minutes to brown the edges, before
removing them and draining on kitchen
paper. Serve warm.

KACHUMBALI SALAD

KACHUMBALI IS A PEPPERY RELISH FROM TANZANIA, WHERE IT IS SERVED WITH GRILLED MEAT OR FISH DISHES, TOGETHER WITH RICE — THIS SALAD USES THE SAME COMBINATION OF VEGETABLES AND FLAVOURS.

SERVES 4–6

INGREDIENTS
 2 red onions
 4 tomatoes
 1 green chilli
 ¹/₂ cucumber
 1 carrot
 juice of 1 lemon
 salt and ground black pepper

1 Slice the onions and tomatoes very thinly and place in a bowl.

2 Slice the chilli lengthways, discard the seeds, then chop very finely. Peel and slice the cucumber and carrot and add to the onions and tomatoes.

3 Squeeze the lemon juice over the salad. Season with salt and freshly ground black pepper and toss together to mix. Serve as an accompaniment, salad or relish.

COOK'S TIP
Traditional *Kachumbali* is made by very finely chopping the onions, tomatoes, cucumber and carrot. This produces a very moist, sauce-like mixture, which is good served inside chapatis and eaten as a snack.

COCONUT CHILLI RELISH

THIS SIMPLE BUT DELICIOUS RELISH IS WIDELY MADE IN TANZANIA. ONLY THE WHITE PART OF THE COCONUT FLESH IS USED — EITHER SHRED IT FAIRLY COARSELY, OR GRATE IT FINELY FOR A MOISTER RESULT.

MAKES ABOUT 50G/2OZ

INGREDIENTS
 50g/2oz fresh or desiccated
  (dry unsweetened shredded) coconut
 10ml/2 tsp lemon juice
 1.5ml/¹/₄ tsp salt
 10ml/2 tsp water
 1.5ml/¹/₄ tsp finely chopped red chilli

1 Grate the coconut and place in a mixing bowl. If using desiccated coconut, add just enough water to moisten it.

2 Add the lemon juice, salt, water and chilli. Stir thoroughly and serve as a relish with meats or as an accompaniment to a main dish.

CHILLI BEAN DIP

THIS CREAMY AND SPICY DIP MADE FROM KIDNEY BEANS IS BEST SERVED WARM WITH TRIANGLES OF GOLDEN BROWN TOASTED PITTA BREAD OR A GENEROUS HELPING OF CRUNCHY TORTILLA CHIPS.

SERVES 4

INGREDIENTS

2 garlic cloves
1 onion
2 fresh green chillies
30ml/2 tbsp vegetable oil
5–10ml/1–2 tsp hot chilli powder
400g/14oz can kidney beans
75g/3oz/¾ cup grated mature (sharp)
  Cheddar cheese
1 red chilli, seeded
salt and ground black pepper

1 Finely chop the garlic and onion. Seed and finely chop the fresh green chillies.

2 Heat the oil in a frying pan and add the garlic, onion, green chillies and chilli powder. Cook gently for 5 minutes, stirring frequently, until the onions are softened.

3 Drain the can of kidney beans, reserving the can juice. Blend all but 30ml/2 tbsp of the beans to a purée in a food processor or blender.

4 Add the puréed beans to the pan with 30–45ml/2–3 tbsp of the reserved can juice. Heat gently, stirring to mix well.

5 Stir in the whole kidney beans and the grated Cheddar cheese. Cook gently for about 2–3 minutes, stirring until all the cheese melts. Add salt and plenty of freshly ground black pepper to taste.

6 Cut the fresh red chilli into tiny strips. Spoon the dip into four individual serving bowls and sprinkle the chilli strips over the top of each one. Serve warm.

COOK'S TIP
For a dip with a coarser texture, do not purée the kidney beans in a food processor or blender; instead, mash them with a potato masher.

CHILLI RELISH

THIS SPICY TOMATO AND RED PEPPER RELISH WILL KEEP FOR AT LEAST A WEEK IN THE REFRIGERATOR. SERVE IT WITH SAUSAGES AND BURGERS IN FRESH WHITE ROLLS WITH A CRISP SALAD.

SERVES 8

INGREDIENTS

6 tomatoes
1 onion
1 red (bell) pepper, seeded
2 garlic cloves
30ml/2 tbsp olive oil
5ml/1 tsp ground cinnamon
5ml/1 tsp chilli flakes
5ml/1 tsp ground ginger
5ml/1 tsp salt
2.5ml/$\frac{1}{2}$ tsp ground black pepper
75g/3oz/$\frac{1}{3}$ cup light muscovado (brown) sugar
75ml/5 tbsp cider vinegar
1 handful of fresh basil leaves

COOK'S TIP
This relish thickens slightly on cooling so don't worry if the mixture seems a little wet at the end of step 5.

1 Skewer each of the tomatoes in turn on a metal fork and hold in a gas flame for 1–2 minutes, turning until the skin splits and wrinkles. Slip off the skins, then coarsely chop the tomatoes.

2 Coarsely chop the onion, red pepper and garlic. Heat the oil in a pan. Add the onion, red pepper and garlic.

3 Cook gently for 5–8 minutes, until the pepper is softened. Add the chopped tomatoes, cover and cook for 5 minutes, until the tomatoes release their juices.

4 Stir in the cinnamon, chilli flakes, ginger, salt, pepper, sugar and vinegar. Bring gently to the boil, stirring until the sugar dissolves.

5 Simmer, uncovered, for approximately 20 minutes, or until the mixture is pulpy. Stir in the basil leaves, and check and adjust the seasoning.

6 Leave the relish to cool completely, then transfer it to a glass jam jar or a plastic container with a tightly fitting lid. Store, covered, in the refrigerator.

SPICED CARROT DIP

THIS IS A DELICIOUS LOW-FAT DIP WITH A SWEET AND SPICY FLAVOUR. SERVE WHEAT CRACKERS OR FIERY TORTILLA CHIPS AS ACCOMPANIMENTS FOR DIPPING.

SERVES 4

INGREDIENTS

1 onion
3 carrots
grated rind and juice of 2 oranges
15ml/1 tbsp hot curry paste
150ml/¼ pint/²/₃ cup low-fat
  natural (plain) yogurt
1 handful of fresh basil leaves
15–30ml/1–2 tbsp fresh lemon juice,
  to taste
red Tabasco sauce, to taste
salt and ground black pepper

1 Using a sharp vegetable knife, finely chop the onion. Peel and grate the carrots. Place the onion, carrots, orange rind and juice and hot curry paste in a small pan. Bring the mixture to the boil, cover with a lid and simmer for about 10 minutes, or until tender.

2 Process the mixture in a blender or food processor until smooth. Leave it to cool completely.

3 Stir in the yogurt, then tear the basil leaves into small pieces and stir them into the carrot mixture.

4 Add lemon juice, Tabasco, salt and pepper to taste and serve.

COOK'S TIP
Use Greek (US strained plain) yogurt or sour cream for a creamier dip.

RED ONION RAITA

Raita is a traditional Indian accompaniment for most hot curries. It is also delicious when served with a pile of spicy poppadums as a dip.

SERVES 4

INGREDIENTS

  5ml/1 tsp cumin seeds
  1 small garlic clove
  1 small green chilli, seeded
  1 large red onion
  150ml/¼ pint/²/₃ cup natural (plain) yogurt
  30ml/2 tbsp chopped fresh coriander
    (cilantro), plus extra to garnish
  2.5ml/½ tsp sugar
  salt

1 Heat a small frying pan and dry-fry the cumin seeds for 1–2 minutes, until they release their aroma and begin to pop.

2 Lightly crush the cumin seeds using a mortar and pestle, or flatten them with the heel of a heavy-bladed knife until they are crushed.

COOK'S TIP
For an extra tangy raita, stir in 15ml/
1 tbsp lemon juice.

3 Finely chop the garlic, green chilli and red onion. Stir them into the yogurt with the crushed cumin seeds and the chopped coriander.

4 Add sugar and salt to taste. Spoon the raita into a small bowl and chill until ready to serve. Garnish with extra coriander before serving.

Warm spices, such as nutmeg, ginger, cinnamon and cardamom, are added to fresh fruit salads, ice creams, pastries, hot desserts and cakes. The selection ranges from Fresh Pineapple with Ginger to wickedly sweet spicy Baklava, from Cinnamon Rolls to Caribbean Fruit and Rum Cake with an Egyptian version of Spiced Bread Pudding and delicious spicy Caramel Rice Pudding.

Sweet and
Spicy Desserts
and Cakes

SPICY NOODLE PUDDING

A traditional Jewish recipe, Spicy Noodle Pudding has a warm aromatic flavour and makes a delicious dessert.

SERVES 4–6

INGREDIENTS

175g/6oz wide egg noodles
225g/8oz/1 cup cottage cheese
115g/4oz/½ cup cream cheese
75g/3oz/scant ½ cup caster
  (superfine) sugar
2 eggs
120ml/4fl oz/½ cup sour cream
5ml/1 tsp vanilla essence (extract)
pinch of ground cinnamon
pinch of grated nutmeg
2.5ml/½ tsp grated lemon rind
50g/2oz/¼ cup butter
25g/1oz/¼ cup nibbed almonds
25g/1oz/scant ½ cup fine dried
  white breadcrumbs
icing (confectioners') sugar for dusting

1 Preheat the oven to 180°C/350°F/Gas 4. Grease a shallow ovenproof dish. Cook the noodles in a large pan of boiling water until just tender. Drain well.

2 Beat the cottage cheese, cream cheese and sugar together in a bowl. Add the eggs, one at a time, and stir in the sour cream. Stir in the vanilla essence, cinnamon, nutmeg and lemon rind.

3 Fold the noodles into the cheese mixture. Spoon into the prepared dish and level the surface.

4 Melt the butter in a frying pan. Add the almonds and cook for about 1 minute. Remove from the heat.

5 Stir in the breadcrumbs, mixing well. Sprinkle the mixture over the pudding. Bake for 30–40 minutes, or until the mixture is set. Serve hot, dusted with a little icing sugar.

AVOCADO SALAD IN GINGER AND ORANGE SAUCE

THIS IS AN UNUSUAL FRUIT SALAD SINCE AVOCADO IS MORE OFTEN TREATED AS A VEGETABLE. HOWEVER, IN THE CARIBBEAN IT IS USED AS A FRUIT, WHICH OF COURSE IT IS!

SERVES 4

INGREDIENTS

2 firm ripe avocados
3 firm ripe bananas, chopped
12 fresh cherries or strawberries
juice of 1 large orange
shredded fresh root ginger

For the ginger syrup
50g/2oz fresh root ginger, chopped
900ml/1½ pints/3¾ cups water
225g/8oz/1 cup demerara (raw) sugar
2 cloves

1 First make the ginger syrup; place the ginger, water, sugar and cloves in a pan and bring to the boil. Reduce the heat and simmer for about 1 hour, until well reduced and syrupy.

2 Remove the ginger and discard. Leave to cool. Store in a covered, clean container in the refrigerator.

3 Peel the avocados, cut into cubes and place in a bowl with the bananas and cherries or strawberries.

4 Pour the orange juice over the fruits. Add 60ml/4 tbsp of the ginger syrup and mix gently, using a metal spoon. Chill for 30 minutes and add a little shredded ginger before serving.

FRESH PINEAPPLE WITH GINGER

THIS REFRESHING DESSERT CAN ALSO BE MADE WITH VACUUM-PACKED PINEAPPLE. THIS MAKES A GOOD SUBSTITUTE, BUT FRESH IS BEST.

SERVES 4

INGREDIENTS
1 fresh pineapple, peeled
slivers of fresh coconut
300ml/½ pint/1¼ cups pineapple juice
60ml/4 tbsp coconut liqueur
2.5cm/1in piece preserved stem ginger,
    plus 45ml/3 tbsp of the syrup

1 Peel and slice the pineapple, arrange in a serving dish and sprinkle the coconut slivers on top.

2 Place the pineapple juice and coconut liqueur in a pan and heat gently.

3 Thinly slice the preserved stem ginger and add to the pan with the syrup. Bring just to the boil and then simmer gently until the liquid is slightly reduced and the sauce is fairly thick.

4 Pour the sauce over the pineapple and coconut. Leave the mixture to cool, then chill before serving.

COOK'S TIP
If fresh coconut is not available, use desiccated (dry unsweetened shredded) coconut instead.

SPICED NUTTY BANANAS

CINNAMON AND NUTMEG ARE SPICES THAT PERFECTLY COMPLEMENT THE BANANAS USED IN THIS DELECTABLE DESSERT.

SERVES 3

INGREDIENTS

6 ripe, but firm, bananas
30ml/2 tbsp chopped unsalted cashew
nuts
30ml/2 tbsp chopped unsalted peanuts
30ml/2 tbsp desiccated (dry
unsweetened shredded) coconut
7.5–15ml/$\frac{1}{2}$–1 tbsp demerara (raw)
sugar
5ml/1 tsp ground cinnamon
2.5ml/$\frac{1}{2}$ tsp freshly grated nutmeg
150ml/$\frac{1}{4}$ pint/$\frac{2}{3}$ cup orange juice
60ml/4 tbsp rum
15g/$\frac{1}{2}$oz/1 tbsp butter or margarine
double (heavy) cream, to serve

1 Preheat the oven to 200°C/400°F/Gas 6. Slice the bananas and place in a greased, shallow ovenproof dish.

2 Mix together the cashew nuts, peanuts, coconut, sugar, cinnamon and nutmeg in a small bowl.

3 Pour the orange juice and rum over the bananas, then sprinkle with the nut and sugar mixture.

4 Dot the top with butter or margarine, then bake in the oven for 15–20 minutes, or until the bananas are golden and the sauce is bubbly. Serve with double cream.

COOK'S TIP
Freshly grated nutmeg makes all the difference to this dish. More rum can be added if you like. Chopped mixed nuts can be used instead of peanuts.

FRUITS OF THE TROPICS SALAD

SERVES 4–6

INGREDIENTS

1 medium pineapple
400g/14oz can guava halves in syrup
2 medium bananas, sliced
1 large mango, peeled, stoned (pitted)
   and diced
115g/4oz preserved stem ginger and
   30ml/2 tbsp of the syrup
60ml/4 tbsp thick coconut milk
10ml/2 tsp sugar
2.5ml/$\frac{1}{2}$ tsp freshly grated nutmeg
2.5ml/$\frac{1}{2}$ tsp ground cinnamon
strips of coconut, to decorate

1 Peel, core and cube the pineapple, and place in a serving bowl. Drain the guavas, reserve the syrup and chop. Add the guavas to the bowl with one of the bananas and the mango.

2 Chop the preserved stem ginger and add to the pineapple mixture.

3 Pour 30ml/2 tbsp of the ginger syrup, and the reserved guava syrup into a blender or food processor and add the other banana, the coconut milk and the sugar. Process to make a smooth creamy purée.

4 Pour the banana and coconut mixture over the fruit, add a little grated nutmeg and a sprinkling of cinnamon. Serve chilled, decorated with strips of coconut.

COCONUT AND NUTMEG ICE CREAM

AN EASY-TO-MAKE, QUITE HEAVENLY, ICE CREAM THAT WILL BE LOVED BY ALL FOR ITS TROPICAL TASTE.

SERVES 8

INGREDIENTS

400g/14oz can evaporated
  (unsweetened condensed) milk
400g/14oz can sweetened
  condensed milk
400g/14oz can coconut milk
freshly grated nutmeg
5ml/1 tsp almond essence (extract)
lemon balm sprigs, lime slices and
  shredded coconut, to decorate

1 Mix together the evaporated, condensed and coconut milks in a large freezerproof bowl and stir in the nutmeg and almond essence.

2 Chill in a freezer for about an hour or two until the mixture is semi-frozen.

3 Remove from the freezer and whisk the mixture with a hand or electric whisk until it is fluffy and almost doubled in volume.

4 Pour into a freezer container, then cover and freeze. Soften slightly before serving, decorated with lemon balm, lime slices and shredded coconut.

BAKLAVA

THIS IS QUEEN OF ALL PASTRIES WITH ITS EXOTIC FLAVOURS AND IS USUALLY SERVED FOR THE PERSIAN NEW YEAR ON MARCH 21, CELEBRATING THE FIRST DAY OF SPRING.

SERVES 6–8

INGREDIENTS
   350g/12oz/3 cups ground
     pistachio nuts
   150g/5oz/1¼ cups icing
     (confectioners') sugar
   15ml/1 tbsp ground cardamom
   150g/5oz/²/₃ cup unsalted (sweet)
     butter, melted
   450g/1lb filo pastry

For the syrup
   450g/1lb/2 cups granulated sugar
   300ml/½ pint/1¼ cups water
   30ml/2 tbsp rose-water

1 First make the syrup: place the sugar and water in a pan, bring to the boil and then simmer for 10 minutes, until syrupy. Stir in the rose-water and leave to cool.

2 Mix together the nuts, icing sugar and cardamom. Preheat the oven to 160°C/325°F/Gas 3 and brush a large rectangular baking tin (pan) with a little melted butter.

3 Taking one sheet of filo pastry at a time, and keeping the remainder covered with a damp cloth, brush with melted butter and lay on the base of the tin. Continue until yoy have six buttered layers in the tin. Spread half of the nut mixture over, pressing down with a spoon.

4 Take another six sheets of filo pastry, brush with butter and lay over the nut mixture. Sprinkle over the remaining nuts and top with a final layer of six filo sheets brushed again with butter. Cut the pastry diagonally into small lozenge shapes using a sharp knife. Pour the remaining melted butter over the top.

5 Bake for 20 minutes, then increase the heat to 200°C/400°F/Gas 6 and bake for 15 minutes, until light golden in colour and puffed.

6 Remove from the oven and drizzle about three-quarters of the syrup over the pastry, reserving the remainder for serving. Arrange the baklava lozenges on a large glass dish and serve with extra syrup.

SPICED BREAD PUDDING

HERE'S A SPICY EGYPTIAN VERSION OF BREAD AND BUTTER PUDDING.

SERVES 4

INGREDIENTS

   10–12 sheets filo pastry
   600ml/1 pint/2½ cups milk
   250ml/8fl oz/1 cup double (heavy)
    cream
   1 egg, beaten
   30ml/2 tbsp rose-water
   50g/2oz/½ cup each chopped
    pistachio nuts, almonds and hazelnuts
   115g/4oz/⅔ cup raisins
   15ml/1 tbsp ground cinnamon
   single (light) cream, to serve

1 Preheat the oven to 160°C/325°F/Gas 3. Bake the filo pastry, on a baking sheet, for 15–20 minutes, until crisp. Remove from the oven and raise the temperature to 200°C/400°F/Gas 6.

2 Scald the milk and cream by pouring into a pan and heating very gently until hot but not boiling. Gradually add the beaten egg and the rose-water. Cook over a very low heat until the mixture begins to thicken, stirring constantly.

3 Crumble the pastry using your hands and then spread in layers with the nuts and raisins into the base of a shallow ovenproof dish.

4 Pour the custard mixture over the nut and pastry base and bake in the oven for 20 minutes, until golden. Sprinkle with cinnamon and serve with single cream.

CARAMEL RICE PUDDING

THIS RICE PUDDING IS DELICIOUS SERVED WITH CRUNCHY FRESH FRUIT.

SERVES 4

INGREDIENTS

50g/2oz/4 tbsp short grain
  pudding rice
75ml/5 tbsp demerara (raw) sugar
5ml/1 tsp ground cinnamon
400g/14oz can evaporated
  (unsweetened condensed) milk
  made up to 600ml/1 pint/2¹/₂ cups
  with water
knob (pat) of butter
1 small fresh pineapple
2 crisp eating apples
10ml/2 tsp lemon juice

1 Preheat the oven to 150°C/300°F/Gas 2. Put the rice in a sieve and wash thoroughly under cold water. Drain well and put into a lightly greased soufflé dish.

2 Add 30ml/2 tbsp sugar and the cinnamon to the dish. Add the diluted milk and stir gently.

3 Dot the surface of the rice with butter and bake for 2 hours, then leave to cool for 30 minutes.

4 Meanwhile, peel, core and slice the pineapple and apples and then cut the pineapple into chunks. Toss the fruit in lemon juice and set aside.

5 Preheat the grill (broiler) and sprinkle the remaining sugar over the rice. Grill (broil) for 5 minutes, or until the sugar has caramelized. Leave the rice to stand for 5 minutes to allow the caramel to harden, then serve with the fresh fruit.

SPICED RICE PUDDING

BOTH MUSLIM AND HINDU COMMUNITIES PREPARE THIS PUDDING, WHICH IS TRADITIONALLY SERVED AT MOSQUES AND TEMPLES.

SERVES 4–6

INGREDIENTS

15ml/1 tbsp ghee or melted unsalted
  (sweet) butter
5cm/2in piece cinnamon stick
225g/8oz/1 cup soft brown sugar
115g/4oz/¹/₂ cup ground rice
1.2 litres/2 pints/5 cups milk
5ml/1 tsp ground cardamom seeds
50g/2oz/scant ¹/₂ cup sultanas
  (golden raisins)
25g/1oz/¹/₄ cup slivered almonds
2.5ml/¹/₂ tsp grated nutmeg, to serve

1 In a heavy pan, heat the ghee or butter and cook the cinnamon and sugar. Keep cooking until the sugar begins to caramelize. Reduce the heat immediately when this happens.

2 Add the rice and half of the milk. Bring to the boil, stirring constantly to avoid the milk boiling over. Reduce the heat and simmer until the rice is cooked, stirring frequently.

3 Add the remaining milk, cardamom, sultanas and almonds and leave to simmer, but keep stirring to prevent the rice from sticking to the base of the pan. When the mixture has thickened, serve hot or cold, sprinkled with grated nutmeg.

DATE AND NUT PASTRIES

MAKES 35–40

INGREDIENTS
  450g/1lb/4 cups plain (all-purpose)
    flour
  225g/8oz/1 cup unsalted (sweet)
    butter, cut into cubes
  45ml/3 tbsp rose-water
  60–75ml/4–5 tbsp milk
  icing (confectioners') sugar, for sprinkling

For the filling
  225g/8oz/1¼ cups dates, pitted
    and chopped
  175g/6oz/1½ cups walnuts,
    finely chopped
  115g/4oz/1 cup blanched
    almonds, chopped
  50g/2oz/½ cup pistachio
    nuts, chopped
  120ml/4fl oz/½ cup water
  115g/4oz/½ cup sugar
  10ml/2 tsp ground cinnamon

1 Preheat the oven to 160°C/325°F/Gas 3. First make the filling: place the dates, walnuts, almonds, pistachios, water, sugar and cinnamon in a small pan and cook over a low heat until the dates are soft and the water has been absorbed.

2 Place the flour in a large bowl and add the butter, working it into the flour with your fingertips.

3 Add the rose-water and milk and knead the dough until it's soft.

4 Take walnut-size lumps of dough. Roll each into a ball and hollow with your thumb. Pinch the sides.

5 Place a spoonful of date mixture in the hollow and then press the dough back over the filling to seal.

6 Arrange the pastries on a large baking sheet. Press to flatten them slightly. Make little dents with a fork on the pastry. Bake in the oven for 20 minutes. Do not let them change colour or the pastry will become hard. Cool slightly and then sprinkle with icing sugar and serve.

CINNAMON BALLS

GROUND ALMONDS OR HAZELNUTS FORM THE BASIS OF MOST PASSOVER CAKES AND BISCUITS. THESE BALLS SHOULD BE SOFT INSIDE, WITH A VERY STRONG CINNAMON FLAVOUR. THEY HARDEN WITH KEEPING, SO IT IS A GOOD IDEA TO FREEZE SOME AND ONLY USE THEM WHEN REQUIRED.

MAKES ABOUT 15

INGREDIENTS
  175g/6oz/1½ cups ground almonds
  75g/3oz/scant ½ cup caster (superfine)
    sugar
  15ml/1 tbsp ground cinnamon
  2 egg whites
  oil, for greasing
  icing (confectioners') sugar, for
    dredging

1 Preheat the oven to 180°C/350°F/Gas 4. Grease a large baking sheet with oil.

2 Mix together the ground almonds, sugar and cinnamon. Whisk the egg whites until they begin to stiffen and fold enough into the almonds to make a fairly firm mixture.

3 Wet your hands with cold water and roll small spoonfuls of the mixture into balls. Place these at intervals on the baking sheet.

4 Bake for about 15 minutes in the centre of the oven. They should be slightly soft inside – too much cooking will make them hard and tough.

5 Slide a spatula under the balls to release them from the baking sheet and leave to cool. Sift a few tablespoons of icing sugar on to a plate and when the cinnamon balls are cold slide them on to the plate. Shake gently to completely cover the cinnamon balls in sugar and store in an airtight container or in the freezer.

APPLE AND CINNAMON CRUMBLE CAKE

THIS SCRUMPTIOUS CAKE HAS LAYERS OF SPICY FRUIT AND CRUMBLE AND IS QUITE DELICIOUS SERVED WARM WITH FRESH CREAM.

MAKES 1 CAKE

INGREDIENTS
- 3 large cooking apples
- 2.5ml/$^{1}/_{2}$ tsp ground cinnamon
- 250g/9oz/1 cup butter
- 250g/9oz/1$^{1}/_{4}$ cups caster (superfine) sugar
- 4 eggs
- 450g/1lb/4 cups self-raising (self-rising) flour

For the crumble topping
- 175g/6oz/$^{3}/_{4}$ cup demerara (raw) sugar
- 125g/4$^{1}/_{4}$ oz/generous 1 cup plain (all-purpose) flour
- 5ml/1 tsp ground cinnamon
- 65g/2$^{1}/_{2}$ oz/about 4$^{1}/_{2}$ tbsp desiccated (dry unsweetened shredded) coconut
- 115g/4oz/$^{1}/_{2}$ cup butter

1 Preheat the oven to 180°C/350°F/Gas 4. Grease a 25cm/10in round cake tin (pan) and line the base with greaseproof (waxed) paper. To make the crumble topping, mix together the sugar, flour, cinnamon and coconut in a bowl, then rub in the butter with your fingertips and set aside.

COOK'S TIP
To make the topping in a food processor, add all the ingredients and process for a few seconds until the mixture resembles bread-crumbs. You can also grate the apples using the grating disc. If you don't have a 25cm/10in round tin, you can use a 20cm/8in square cake tin.

2 Peel and core the apples, then grate them coarsely. Place them in a bowl, sprinkle with the cinnamon and set aside.

3 Cream the butter and sugar in a bowl with an electric mixer, until light and fluffy. Beat in the eggs, one at a time, beating well after each addition.

4 Sift in half the flour, mix well, then add the remaining flour and stir until smooth.

5 Spread half the cake mixture evenly over the base of the prepared tin. Spoon the apples on top and sprinkle over half the crumble topping.

6 Spread the remaining cake mixture over the crumble and finally top with the remaining crumble topping.

7 Bake for 1 hour 10 minutes to 1 hour 20 minutes, covering the cake with foil if it browns too quickly. Leave in the tin for about 5 minutes, before turning out on to a wire rack. Once cool, cut into slices to serve.

BANANA GINGER CAKE

MAKES 1 CAKE

INGREDIENTS
- 200g/7oz/1³/4 cups plain (all-purpose) flour
- 10ml/2 tsp bicarbonate of soda (baking soda)
- 10ml/2 tsp ground ginger
- 150g/5oz/1¹/4 cups medium oatmeal
- 60ml/4 tbsp dark muscovado (molasses) sugar
- 75g/3oz/6 tbsp sunflower margarine
- 150g/5oz/³/4 cup golden (light corn) syrup
- 1 egg, beaten
- 3 ripe bananas, mashed
- 75g/3oz/³/4 cup icing (confectioners') sugar
- preserved stem ginger, to decorate

1 Preheat the oven to 160°C/325°F/Gas 3. Grease and line an 18 x 28cm/7 x 11in cake tin.

2 Stir together the flour, bicarbonate of soda and ginger, then stir in the oatmeal. Heat the sugar, margarine and golden syrup in a pan, until melted, then stir into the flour mixture. Beat in the egg and mashed bananas.

3 Spoon into the tin and bake for about 1 hour, or until firm to the touch. Leave the cake to cool in the tin, then turn out and cut into squares.

4 Sift the icing sugar into a bowl and stir in just enough water to make a smooth, runny icing. Drizzle the icing over each square and top with a piece of preserved stem ginger.

COOK'S TIP
This is a nutritious, energy-giving cake that is a really good choice for packed lunches because it doesn't break up too easily.

SPICED DATE AND WALNUT CAKE

MIXED SPICE ADDS A WARM FLAVOUR TO THIS LOW-FAT, HIGH-FIBRE CAKE. SIMPLY SERVE IT ON ITS OWN,
OR SPREAD IT WITH BUTTER AND HONEY FOR AN EXTRA SPECIAL SNACK.

MAKES 1 CAKE

INGREDIENTS

300g/11oz/2²/₃ cups wholemeal
  (whole-wheat) self-raising (self-
  rising) flour
10ml/2 tsp mixed (apple pie) spice
150g/5oz/scant 1 cup chopped dates
50g/2oz/¹/₂ cup chopped walnuts
60ml/4 tbsp sunflower oil
115g/4oz/¹/₂ cup dark muscovado sugar
300ml/¹/₂ pint/1¹/₄ cups skimmed milk
walnut halves, to decorate

VARIATION
Pecan nuts can be used in place of
the walnuts in this cake, if you like.

1 Preheat the oven to 180°C/350°F/Gas 4.
Grease and line a 900g/2lb loaf tin (pan)
with greaseproof (waxed) paper.

2 Sift together the self-raising flour and
mixed spice, adding back any bran from
the sieve. Stir in the dates and walnuts.

3 Mix the oil, sugar and milk, then add to
the dry ingredients. Mix well, then spoon
the mixture into the prepared tin.

4 Arrange the walnut halves over the top
of the cake mixture. Bake the cake for
45–50 minutes, or until golden brown and
firm. Turn out the cake, remove the lining
paper and leave to cool on a wire rack.

CINNAMON ROLLS

MAKES 24 SMALL ROLLS

INGREDIENTS
For the dough
    400g/14oz/3$\frac{1}{2}$ cups strong white flour
    2.5ml/$\frac{1}{2}$ tsp salt
    30ml/2 tbsp sugar
    5ml/1 tsp easy-blend (rapid-rise) dried yeast
    45ml/3 tbsp oil
    1 egg
    120ml/4fl oz/$\frac{1}{2}$ cup warm milk
    120ml/4fl oz/$\frac{1}{2}$ cup warm water

For the filling
    25g/1oz/2 tbsp butter, softened
    25g/1oz/2 tbsp dark brown sugar
    2.5–5ml/$\frac{1}{2}$–1 tsp ground cinnamon
    15ml/1 tbsp raisins

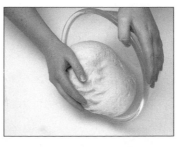

1 Sift the flour, salt and sugar and sprinkle over the yeast. Mix the oil, egg, milk and water and add to the flour. Mix to a dough, then knead until smooth. Leave to rise until doubled in size and then knock back (punch down).

2 Roll out the dough into a large rectangle and cut in half vertically. Spread over the soft butter, reserving 15ml/1 tbsp for brushing. Mix the sugar and cinnamon and sprinkle over the top. Dot the dough with the raisins.

3 Roll each piece into a long Swiss (jelly) roll shape, to enclose the filling. Cut into 2.5cm/1in slices, arrange flat on a greased baking sheet and brush with the remaining butter. Leave to rise again for about 30 minutes.

4 Preheat the oven to 200°C/400°F/Gas 6 and bake the cinnamon rolls for about 20 minutes. Leave to cool on a wire rack. Serve fresh for breakfast or tea, with extra butter if you like.

PEACH KUCHEN

THE JOY OF THIS CAKE IS ITS ALL-IN-ONE SIMPLICITY. IT CAN BE SERVED STRAIGHT FROM THE OVEN, OR CUT INTO SQUARES WHEN COLD.

SERVES 8

INGREDIENTS

   350g/12oz/3 cups self-raising
    (self-rising) flour
   225g/8oz/1 cup caster (superfine)
    sugar
   175g/6oz/³⁄₄ cup unsalted (sweet)
    butter, softened
   2 eggs
   120ml/4fl oz/¹⁄₂ cup milk
   6 large peeled peaches, sliced or
    450g/1lb plums or cherries, pitted
   115g/4oz/¹⁄₂ cup soft brown sugar
   2.5ml/¹⁄₂ tsp ground cinnamon
   sour cream or crème fraîche, to serve

1 Preheat the oven to 190°C/375°F/Gas 5. Grease and line a 20 x 25 x 2.5cm/8 x 10 x 1in cake tin (pan).

2 Put the flour, sugar, butter, eggs and milk into a large bowl and beat for a few minutes until you have a smooth batter. Spoon it into the prepared cake tin.

COOK'S TIP
To peel ripe peaches, cover with boiling water for 20 seconds. The skin will then slip off easily.

3 Arrange the peaches, plums or cherries over the cake mixture. Mix the brown sugar and cinnamon and sprinkle it over the fruit.

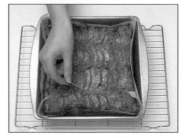

4 Bake for about 40 minutes, testing for doneness by inserting a cocktail stick (toothpick) in the centre.

5 Serve the cake warm or cool with the sour cream or crème fraîche.

CARIBBEAN FRUIT AND RUM CAKE

THIS IS A DELICIOUS RECIPE FOR A CAKE THAT IS EATEN AT CHRISTMAS, WEDDINGS AND OTHER SPECIAL OCCASIONS. IT IS KNOWN AS BLACK CAKE, BECAUSE, TRADITIONALLY, THE RECIPE USES BURNT SUGAR.

MAKES 1 CAKE

INGREDIENTS
  450g/1lb/2 cups currants
  450g/1lb/3 cups raisins
  225g/8oz/1 cup prunes, pitted
  115g/4oz/²/₃ cup mixed (candied) peel
  400g/14oz/2¼ cups dark soft brown sugar
  5ml/1 tsp mixed (apple pie) spice
  90ml/6 tbsp rum, plus more if needed
  300ml/½ pint/1¼ cups sherry, plus
    more if needed
  450g/1lb/2 cups softened butter
  10 eggs, beaten
  450g/1lb/4 cups self-raising
    (self-rising) flour
  5ml/1 tsp vanilla essence (extract)

2 Stir the fruit mixture occasionally and keep covered, adding more alcohol, if you like.

5 Add the fruit mixture, then gradually stir in the flour and vanilla essence. Mix well, adding 15–30ml/1–2 tbsp sherry if the mixture is too stiff; it should just fall off the back of the spoon, but should not be too runny.

1 Wash the currants, raisins, prunes and mixed peel, then pat dry. Place in a food processor and process until finely chopped. Transfer to a large, clean jar or bowl, add 115g/4oz of the sugar, the mixed spice, rum and sherry. Mix very well and then cover with a lid and set aside for anything from 2 weeks to 3 months – the longer it is left, the better the flavour will be.

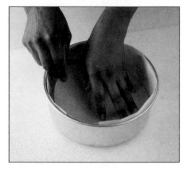

3 Preheat the oven to 160°C/325°F/Gas 3. Grease and line a 25cm/10in round cake tin (pan) with a double layer of greaseproof (waxed) paper.

4 Sift the flour and set aside. Cream together the butter and remaining sugar and beat in the eggs until the mixture is smooth and creamy.

6 Spoon the mixture into the prepared tin, cover loosely with foil and bake for about 2½ hours, until the cake is firm and springy. Leave to cool in the tin overnight, then sprinkle with more rum if the cake is not to be used immediately. Wrap the cake in foil to keep it moist.

COOK'S TIP
Although the dried fruits are chopped in a food processor, they can be marinated whole, if you prefer. If you don't have enough time to marinate the fruit, simmer the fruit in the alcohol mixture for about 30 minutes, and leave overnight.

Spices are added to a wide range of drinks and

Sangrita, from Mexico, even uses fresh green

chillies! Cocktails such as Bloody Maria are

pepped up with Worcestershire and Tabasco

sauces, while Caribbean punches, including

Caribbean Cream Stout Punch, are enlivened

with a sprinkling of spice. Mulled Wine and

Spiced Mocha Drink are hot favourites too.

Spiced Drinks

SPICED MOCHA DRINK

THIS SPICY CHOCOLATE MILK DRINK CAN BE SERVED EITHER HOT OR COLD — DEPENDING ON THE WEATHER AND YOUR PREFERENCE.

SERVES 4

INGREDIENTS
175g/6oz milk chocolate
120ml/4fl oz/¹/₂ cup single (light)
   cream
750ml/1¹/₄ pints/3 cups hot
   black coffee
2.5ml/¹/₂ tsp ground cinnamon
whipped cream or ice, to serve

1 Using a sharp knife, cut the chocolate into small pieces to enable it to melt quickly and evenly.

2 Put the chocolate into a double saucepan or a bowl set over a pan of almost simmering water. The base of the bowl should not touch the water.

3 Add the single cream to the chocolate melting in the bowl, then stir well to mix.

4 Continue to heat gently until the chocolate is melted and smooth, stirring occasionally. Remove the bowl from the heat.

5 Add the coffee and cinnamon to the chocolate and whisk until foamy. Divide among four serving glasses, then either serve hot with a spoonful of cream, or cool and chill, and serve over ice.

COOK'S TIP
If any steam gets into the chocolate while you are melting it, it may turn into a solid mass. If this happens, stir in about 5ml/1 tsp butter or margarine for each 25g/1oz of chocolate.

MULLED WINE

CLOVES, CINNAMON AND NUTMEG ADD SPICY FLAVOUR TO THIS DELICIOUS MULLED WINE.
IT MAKES A WARMING DRINK FOR A WINTER PARTY.

MAKES 16 × 150ml/¼ PINT/⅔ CUP GLASSES

INGREDIENTS
1 orange
60ml/4 tbsp demerara (raw) sugar
grated nutmeg
2 cinnamon sticks
a few cloves, plus extra for studding
30ml/2 tbsp seedless raisins
75ml/5 tbsp clear honey
2 clementines
1.5 litres/2½ pints/6¼ cups red wine
750ml/1¼ pints/3 cups medium
   (hard) cider
300ml/½ pint/1¼ cups orange juice

VARIATION
Vary the spices used in this mulled
wine – whole allspice can be added
instead of cinnamon sticks. If you
like, you can also add a selection of
sliced citrus fruits.

1 With a sharp knife or a vegetable peeler,
pare off a long strip of orange rind.

2 Place the sugar, nutmeg, cinnamon,
cloves, raisins, honey and rind in a large
pan. Stud the clementines with cloves and
add them to the pan. Add the wine and
heat gently until the sugar is dissolved.
Pour in the cider and continue to heat
gently. Do not boil.

3 Add the orange juice to the pan and
warm through. Remove the clementines
and cinnamon sticks and strain the
mulled wine into a warmed punch bowl or
other serving bowl. Add the clove-studded
clementines and serve hot in warmed
glasses, or in glasses containing a small
spoon (to prevent the glass from
breaking).

SANGRITA

INGREDIENTS
   450g/1lb tomatoes, peeled, seeded
      and chopped
   120ml/4fl oz/½ cup orange juice
   60ml/4 tbsp freshly squeezed lime juice
   1 small onion, chopped
   2.5ml/½ tsp granulated sugar
   6 small fresh green chillies, seeded
      and chopped
   50ml/2oz aged tequila *(Tequila Anejo)*
      per person
   salt

COOK'S TIP
Plain white tequila is not suitable for
this. Choose one of the amber aged
tequilas *(Añejos)*, which are smoother
and more gentle on the palate.

1 Put the chopped tomatoes, orange
juice, lime juice, chopped onion,
granulated sugar and chopped green
chillies into a food processor.

2 Process the tomato mixture until very
smooth, scraping down the sides if
necessary.

3 Pour the tomato mixture into a jug
(pitcher) and chill well.

4 To serve, pour into small glasses,
allowing about 90ml/6 tbsp per portion.
Pour the tequila into separate small
glasses. Sip the tomato juice and tequila
alternately.

SANGRIA

*This very popular summer drink was borrowed from Spain. The Mexican version is slightly less
alcoholic than the original.*

INGREDIENTS
   ice cubes
   1 litre/1¾ pints/4 cups dry red
      table wine
   150ml/¼ pint/⅔ cup freshly squeezed
      orange juice
   50ml/2fl oz/¼ cup freshly squeezed
      lime juice
   115g/4oz/generous ½ cup caster
      (superfine) sugar
   2 limes or 1 apple, sliced, to serve

1 Half fill a large jug (pitcher) with ice
cubes. Pour in the wine and the orange
and lime juices.

2 Add the sugar and stir well until it has
dissolved. Pour into tall glasses and float
the lime or apple slices on top. Serve
immediately.

COOK'S TIP
Sugar does not dissolve readily in
alcohol. It is easier to use simple
syrup, which is very easy to make and
gives a smoother drink. Combine
475ml/16fl oz/2 cups granulated
sugar and 450g/1lb water in a jug
(pitcher) and set aside until the sugar
has dissolved. Stir from time to time.
15ml/1 tbsp simple syrup is the
equivalent of 7.5ml/1½ tsp sugar.

BLOODY MARIA

SERVES 2

INGREDIENTS
175ml/6fl oz/¾ cup tomato juice
90ml/3fl oz/6 tbsp white tequila
dash each of Worcestershire and
    Tabasco sauces
30ml/2 tbsp lemon juice
salt and ground black pepper
8 ice cubes

COOK'S TIP
When drinks are to be served with ice,
make sure all the ingredients are
thoroughly chilled ahead of time.

1 Combine the tomato juice, tequila,
Worcestershire and Tabasco sauces, and
lemon juice in a cocktail shaker. Add salt
and pepper to taste, and four ice cubes.
Shake very vigorously.

2 Place the remaining ice cubes in two
heavy-based glasses and strain the tequila
over them.

MARGARITA

*TEQUILA IS MADE FROM THE SAP OF A FLESHY-LEAFED PLANT CALLED THE BLUE AGAVE AND GETS ITS NAME
FROM THE TOWN OF TEQUILA, WHERE IT HAS BEEN MADE FOR MORE THAN 200 YEARS. THE MARGARITA IS
THE MOST POPULAR AND BEST-KNOWN DRINK MADE WITH TEQUILA.*

SERVES 2

INGREDIENTS
½ lime or lemon
120ml/4fl oz/½ cup white tequila
30ml/2 tbsp Triple Sec or Cointreau
30ml/2 tbsp freshly squeezed lime or
    lemon juice
4 or more ice cubes
salt

1 Rub the rims of two cocktail glasses
with the lime or lemon. Pour some salt
into a saucer and dip in the glasses so
that the rims are frosted.

2 Combine the tequila, Triple Sec or
Cointreau, and lime and lemon juice in a
jug (pitcher) and stir to mix well.

3 Pour the tequila mixture into the
prepared glasses. Add the ice cubes and
serve immediately.

COOK'S TIP
It really is worth going to the trouble
of buying limes for this recipe.
Lemons will do, but something of the
special flavour of the drink will be lost
in the substitution.

DEMERARA RUM PUNCH

THE INSPIRATION FOR THIS PUNCH CAME FROM THE RUM DISTILLERY AT PLANTATION DIAMOND ESTATE IN GUYANA WHERE SOME OF THE FINEST RUM IN THE WORLD IS MADE, AND THE TANTALIZING AROMAS OF SUGAR CANE AND RUM PERVADE THE AIR.

SERVES 4

INGREDIENTS

150ml/¼ pint/²/₃ cup orange juice
150ml/¼ pint/²/₃ cup pineapple juice
150ml/¼ pint/²/₃ cup mango juice
120ml/4fl oz/½ cup water
250ml/8fl oz/1 cup dark rum
a dash of angostura bitters
freshly grated nutmeg
25g/1 oz/2 tbsp demerara (raw) sugar
1 small banana
1 large orange

COOK'S TIP

You can use white rum instead of dark, if you prefer. To make a stronger punch, add more rum.

1 Pour the orange, pineapple and mango juices into a large punch bowl, then stir in the water.

2 Add the rum, angostura bitters, nutmeg and sugar. Stir gently for a few minutes until the sugar has dissolved.

3 Slice the banana and stir gently into the punch.

4 Slice the orange and add to the punch. Chill and serve with ice.

CARIBBEAN CREAM STOUT PUNCH

A WELL-KNOWN "PICK-ME-UP" THAT IS POPULAR ALL OVER THE CARIBBEAN.

SERVES 2

INGREDIENTS
475ml/16fl oz/2 cups stout
300ml/¹/₂ pint/1¹/₄ cups evaporated
  (unsweetened condensed) milk
75ml/5 tbsp sweetened condensed milk
75ml/5 tbsp sherry
2 or 3 drops vanilla essence (extract)
freshly grated nutmeg

1 Mix together the stout, evaporated and condensed milks, sherry and vanilla essence in a blender or food processor, or whisk together in a large mixing bowl, until creamy.

2 Add a little grated nutmeg to the stout mixture and blend or whisk again for a few minutes.

3 Chill for at least 45 minutes until really cold before serving.

INDEX